THANK
YOU
FOR RE-
TURNING
YOUR
BOOKS
ON
TIME!

DATE DUE		
OCT 1 0 '01		
NOV 0 7 '09		
SEP 2 9 2010		
JA 2 9 '14		
FEB 1 2 2014		

COUNTRY STUDIES

SOUTH AFRICA

Garrett Nagle

Series Editor: John Hopkins

Heinemann Library
Chicago, Illinois

©1999 Reed Educational & Professional Publishing
Published by Heinemann Library,
an imprint of Reed Educational & Professional Publishing,
100 North LaSalle, Suite 1010
Chicago, IL 60602
Customer Service: 888-454-2279
Visit our website at www.heinemannlibrary.com

© Garrett Nagle
For Angela, Rosie and Patrick
03 02 01 00
10 9 8 7 6 5 4 3 2

Printed in Hong Kong

Library of Congress Cataloging-in-Publication Data
Nagle, Garrett.
     South Africa / Garrett Nagle.
       p. cm. – (Country studies)
     Summary: Describes the history, geography, population, ecosystems, economic development, politics, and natural resources of South Africa.
     Includes index.
     ISBN 1-57572-896-6 (library binding)
     [1. South Africa--Juvenile literature.] I. Title. II. Series:
Country studies (Des Plaines, Ill.)
DT1719.N34   1999
968—dc21   98-52756
                                       CIP
                                       AP

Acknowledgments

The publishers would like to thank the following for permission to reproduce copyright material.
Maps and extracts
p.5, p.40 Jutas General School Atlas, 1996, Juta & Co., South Africa Atlas; p.10 Reed International; p.11 Development Bank of Southern Africa; p.14 Barnard, Smit and Van Zyl (after Jordaan); p.25 *Geographical Magazine*; p.27 Whitehead & O'Donovan (HSRC); p.30 Paul Chapman Publishing, London; p.33 © Crown Copyright Ordnance Survey; p.38 Reed International; p.39 *Financial Times*; p.40 Consolidated Gold Fields; p.52 *Financial Times*; p.53 Geographical; p.57 Heinemann Educational.
Photographs
p.6 (left) SIPA-Press/Rex Features; p.6 (bottom) N. Durrell McKenna/Hutchison Library; p.7(left) Richard Lord/Rex Features; p.14 SIPA-Press/Rex Features; p.16 Tim Lambon/Environmental Images; p.17 Paul Weinberg/Panos Pictures; p.18 Bradley Arden/Panos Pictures; p.30 (top) Chris Sattleberger/Panos Pictures; p.30 (bottom) Mark Peters/Rex Features; p.33 Axis; p.39 Charles Ward/Camera Press; p.41 Rodney Bond/Camera Press; p.43 (left) Jan Kope/Camera Press; p.43 (right) Paul Weinberg/Panos Pictures; p.44 Burman/Hutchison Library; p.46 Daphne Christelis/Environmental Images; p.47 Vanessa Burger/Images of Africa Photobank; p.48 Gareth Boden; p.52 Clive Shirley/Environmental Images; p.54 David Reed/Panos Pictures; p.55 (top) M. Kahn/Hutchison Library; p.55 (middle) Geoslides; p.58 Anders Gunnartz/Panos Pictures; p.5 SIPA-Press/Rex Features; all other photographs courtesy of the author.
Cover: Getty Images; Eye Ubiquitous/Skjold

Some words are shown in bold, **like this**.
You can find out what they mean by looking in the glossary.

Contents

1 INTRODUCING SOUTH AFRICA

A World in One Country

▶ **South Africa is the tip of Africa.**

▶ **It is a land of contrasts.**

South Africa is a large country. It stretches from **latitude** 22° south to nearly 35° south, and from **longitude** 33° east to 17° east. It covers an area of 470,693 square miles, which is about midway between the land areas of Texas and Alaska.

South Africa is also a varied country. There are great contrasts in relief and distances from the sea, as well as latitude. These cause big variations in the climate and vegetation. South Africa has a mixture of desert and semi-desert, grassland, Mediterranean, mountain, and subtropical environments.

There are nine provinces in South Africa. The smallest one, Gauteng, contains the cities of Johannesburg and Pretoria. By contrast, the largest provinces, such as the Northern Cape, contain large areas of desert.

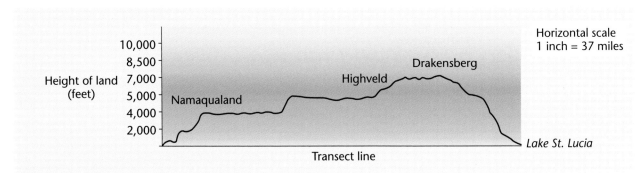

This cross-section graph shows the variation in elevation across the middle of South Africa.

FACT FILE

Map projections

Although the earth is a spherical body, maps show it as a two-dimensional object, with linear scales for latitude and longitude. This has the effect of increasing the relative importance of some areas, such as Greenland, and reducing the importance of others, especially African countries, such as South Africa. Other projections, such as the Mollweide and the Sanson-Flamsteed, have cylindrical scales, which reduce the importance of polar areas and give greater consideration to tropical areas.

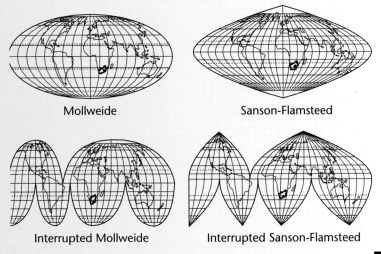

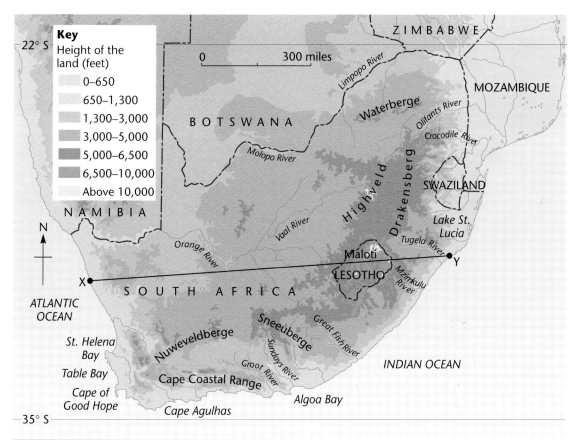

A Physical Map of South Africa

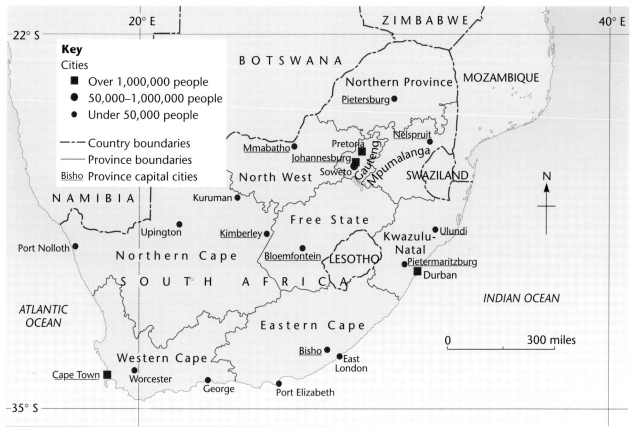

The Nine Provinces of South Africa

Perceptions of South Africa

▶ Not everyone has the same opinion about South Africa.
▶ Perceptions and experiences account for the many viewpoints.

A tourist

South Africa was fantastic. It was inexpensive, the beaches were excellent, the weather was hot and sunny, and there was so much to do and to see. We visited Kruger National Park and saw the "big five": lion, rhino, elephant, buffalo, leopard. We also went to Cape Town and toured along the wine route, and we even did a tour of a **township**. Some people warned us that it would be dangerous, but we did not have any problems. If you keep out of those areas it's fine. I can't wait to go back.

Elephants are one of the "big five" animals to see.

Rugby is a popular game similar to American football.

A school boy after a rugby tour

We had a great rugby tour. We played at a number of schools, and they really looked after us well. The standard of their sport is very high. Most of the time our A-team was playing a mixture of their As and Bs—and they still won most of the matches! The ground was very hard, and they were great tacklers. We were treated very well, and stayed at the students' homes.

A young South African couple who have moved to London

We had to leave. The crime rate was going up and up. It's no place to bring up our children. Cars are being held up in broad daylight in city centers. It used to be just in the townships, but now it's all over. Maybe it's better in small towns and in the countryside, but we can't afford to live there because there aren't any jobs! All the jobs are in Johannesburg.

A security system is in place in Johannesburg.

An Eastern Cape resident

We don't want any more promises. We are sick of all that talk. We need jobs, houses, clinics, schools, and running water, not words. That's why I voted for the government. But what have they done for us? Nothing! Why should the whites still have all South Africa's riches? We are all South Africans.

Poor land and housing exist in the Eastern Cape.

It is debated whether foreign investment in South Africa is exploitation or an economic cure.

An investor

South Africa is an exciting new market, and it's got inroads into the rest of southern Africa. We are keen to invest there. There is a great deal of talent in the population. There is a real buzz of progress in the new South Africa. As people become better off the market will expand. We want to be in there first.

FACT FILE

Perception

People base their views on what they think exists rather than what actually exists. This is their **perception**. Sometimes a person's perception can be very close to reality, other times it bears little resemblance to reality. In general, we would expect that the more experience a person has, the closer to reality his or her perception will be.

Someone who has not been to South Africa will have a very limited understanding of life in South Africa compared with someone living there. In addition, among South Africans, a white person's perception of the country will differ from that of a black person's perception. This is a result of education, experience, class, economic status, and outlook.

In some cases people's perceptions are limited because of the constraints within which they live. A person who cannot read or write, and/or someone who has suffered physical or mental assault and has been denied access to education or health care, will have a different view on the possibilities and the constraints of living in a society, compared with someone who has not been **discriminated** against.

In South Africa, there are clear racial variations in the perception of opportunity and quality of life.

South Africa and Apartheid

▶ South Africa's history has influenced its geography.
▶ The apartheid policy of segregation has ended.

Apartheid was a policy of racial **segregation** that helped the white minority to keep political power. Between 1948 and 1994, the white National Party used apartheid to **discriminate** against the rest of the population. Today, the population of 40 million people is of varied descent.

The effects of apartheid

However, racism and discrimination had existed in South Africa long before 1948. Discrimination took place at different levels.
- At the national level, areas called **homelands** were created and large numbers of black people were forced to live in them.
- At an **urban** level, separate **townships**, sometimes called **locations**, were created for black people, colored people, and Indians. The housing of these townships was always of poorer quality than the housing available for whites.
- Beaches, trains, parks, hospitals, and post offices were segregated by race. It was illegal for black people to use white facilities.

Apartheid forcibly removed millions of black people from designated white farmlands and white areas of towns. They were moved into the homelands and townships. In the homelands, new shanty towns were created, but many of them were very far from the nearest town or city. These plans of action were called **resettlement plans** or **peri-urban** settlements.

In the peri-urban settlements, facilities such as schools, health care, water, sanitation, and transportation were rudimentary. Most of the people in these places were very poor and did not have much opportunity for getting a job. So the younger men **migrated** to "white" South Africa to work in the mines and factories, while the elderly, children, women, and infirmed remained in the homelands.

The end of apartheid

The apartheid regime was ended in 1994 with South Africa's first democratic election. All South Africans were able to vote for the first time. The result was that South Africa's first black president, Nelson Mandela, was elected.

This housing in the black township of Zwelitsha, Eastern Cape is the result of an apartheid policy.

This resettlement is in Glenmore, Eastern Cape.

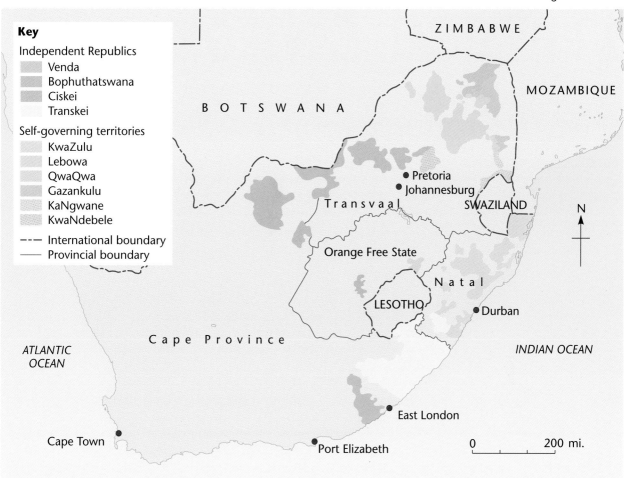

Key

Independent Republics
- Venda
- Bophuthatswana
- Ciskei
- Transkei

Self-governing territories
- KwaZulu
- Lebowa
- QwaQwa
- Gazankulu
- KaNgwane
- KwaNdebele

- --- International boundary
- — Provincial boundary

ZIMBABWE

MOZAMBIQUE

BOTSWANA

• Pretoria
• Johannesburg

T r a n s v a a l

SWAZILAND

N

Orange Free State

N a t a l

LESOTHO

• Durban

Cape Province

ATLANTIC OCEAN

INDIAN OCEAN

East London

Cape Town

Port Elizabeth

0   200 mi.

This map shows the locations of South Africa's homelands in 1993. These areas were set aside for black people.

NELSON MANDELA, *LONG WALK TO FREEDOM*, 1994

I saw my mission as one of preaching reconciliation, of mending the wounds of the country. I knew that many people, particularly the minorities—whites, coloreds, and Indians—would be feeling anxious about the future, and I wanted them to feel secure.

FACT FILE

Dismantling apartheid

The South African government was put under a great deal of pressure by a number of governments and human rights organizations to end apartheid. Trade **sanctions** and divestment (the withdrawal of investment by foreign companies operating in South Africa) added pressure to the government to change.

However, the biggest challenge came from within South Africa, from among the black population and some liberal whites. Politically, the African National Congress (ANC) and the KwaZulu-dominated Inkatha group created a vocal political and military opposition. The churches of South Africa and the trade union movements also added their weight to the calls for a democratic future for all South Africans.

Between 1989 and 1994 apartheid was dismantled. Nelson Mandela was elected President of the Republic of South Africa following the first multiracial democratic elections in South Africa in 1994.

The Effect of Geographic Relief

▶ **Mountains, plateaus, and plains are South Africa's main relief features.**
▶ **The mountains influence the climate and the vegetation.**

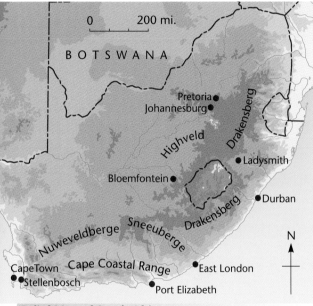

Relief Map of South Africa

South Africa has a number of important mountain ranges, including the Drakensberg, the Cape Coastal Range, the Sneeuberge, and the Nuweveldberge. Much of the rest of South Africa is on a high **plateau** known as the **Highveld**.

Relief, or the height and shape of the land, has an important influence on climate in South Africa. In general, rainfall decreases from east to west, and over half of the country receives less than 10 inches of rain each year. Much of this rain is **relief rainfall**. As the air is forced to rise over a mountain, it cools and **condenses**. Clouds form and rain falls. For example, at the base of the Drakensberg, near Ladysmith, annual rainfall is between 28 and 40 inches. At the top of the mountain it is almost 80 inches. Around Cape Town, rainfall in the lowland areas is just 16 inches. But in the mountains near Stellenbosch, less than 45 miles away, it is as high as 120 inches each year.

Relief and slopes also affect the type of farming. On steep land, only rough grazing is possible. But in the flatter areas it is possible to grow crops where there is enough water.

In some areas, there are many sudden changes in relief. For example, in the Eastern Cape near Bisho, there are four main zones: a coastal plain, a deeply eroded plateau, a lowland basin, and the mountain belt. These have an important impact on local soils, weather, and vegetation patterns.

For example, temperatures decrease with **altitude**. On average, for every 3,200 feet of height, the temperature decreases by 50°F. So high mountain areas can be very cold, making agriculture more difficult.

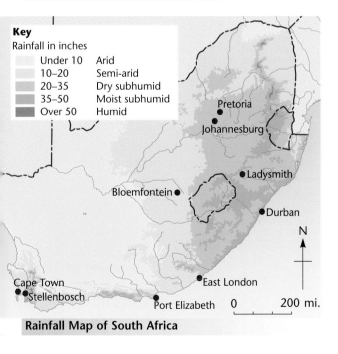

Key

Rainfall in inches

Under 10	Arid
10–20	Semi-arid
20–35	Dry subhumid
35–50	Moist subhumid
Over 50	Humid

Rainfall Map of South Africa

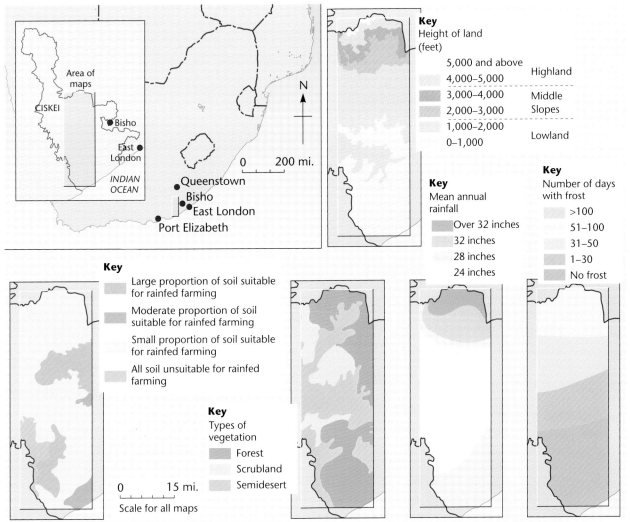

Key
Height of land (feet)

5,000 and above
4,000–5,000 — Highland
3,000–4,000
2,000–3,000 — Middle Slopes
1,000–2,000
0–1,000 — Lowland

Key
Mean annual rainfall

Over 32 inches
32 inches
28 inches
24 inches

Key
Number of days with frost

>100
51–100
31–50
1–30
No frost

Key
Large proportion of soil suitable for rainfed farming
Moderate proportion of soil suitable for rainfed farming
Small proportion of soil suitable for rainfed farming
All soil unsuitable for rainfed farming

Key
Types of vegetation
Forest
Scrubland
Semidesert

0   15 mi.
Scale for all maps

These maps show the relief, soils, vegetation, rainfall, and days of frost in an area near Bisho, Ciskei.

FACT FILE

South Africa in relief

South Africa has three main topographic areas—the interior plateau containing large areas of land with an average elevation of 3,900 feet; the marginal lands lying between the plateau and the coast; and the Great Escarpment forming the border between the plateau and the rugged marginal lands.

The highest peaks within South Africa are in the Escarpment: Mont-aux-Sources at 7,869 feet, Champagne Castle at 11,073 feet, and Giant's Castle at 10,866 feet. The highest point in southern Africa is Thabana-Ntlengana at 11,420 feet, also in the Great Escarpment. But this point is not in South Africa, as it is located within Lesotho, a country entirely surrounded by South Africa.

Key
Kalahan Basin
Plateau
Marginal lands
Coastal plains
Mountains of the Great Escarpment
Other mountains

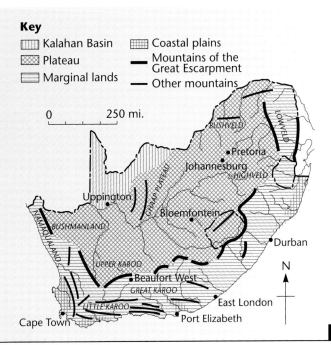

▶ **South Africa has many climates.**
▶ **Its climate varies in different seasons and in different parts of the country.**

South Africa is a country of many climates. The climate varies from place to place, as well as from season to season.

- Rainfall is higher in the mountains due to relief rainfall.
- Rainfall decreases from east to west.
- Most of the rainfall is in the southern hemisphere's summer, from October to March.
- The Cape Town area has rainfall in the southern hemisphere's winter, from April to September.
- Temperatures increase away from the sea and northwards towards the Equator.
- Temperatures are higher in lowland areas and cooler in the highlands.

The city of Durban has a **subtropical** climate beause of the warm Agulhas current. Summer temperatures are warm (68°F–77°F) and the air is **humid**. Winters are warm (60°F–65°F) and frost free. Rainfall is about 40 inches, with 70 percent of it falling during the summer months. Some of this rainfall is heavy and causes **soil erosion.**

By contrast, Johannesburg is located on the **Highveld**. Summers are warm (about 68°F), although sometimes the temperatures can be much higher (86°F). Winters are mild (46°F–50°F), but the nights are very cold, and frosts are common. Temperatures are lower partly because of altitude. Up to 85 percent of the rainfall occurs during the summer. Total annual rainfall is just over 32 inches. **Convection storms** (thunderstorms) produce heavy rain and can cause local flooding.

The southwest corner of South Africa has a **Mediterranean climate.** Unlike other parts of the country, it has winter (April–September) rainfall. Rainfall is moderate, about 24 inches, but can be as high as 120 inches in the mountains. Temperatures range from around 68°F in the summer to 59°F in winter. This is because the sea helps to cool the coast in summer and helps to warm it in winter.

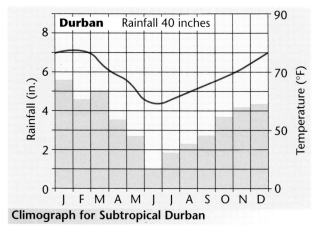

Climograph for Subtropical Durban

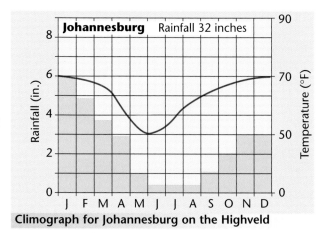

Climograph for Johannesburg on the Highveld

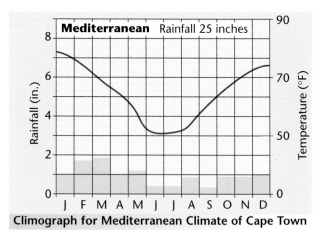

Climograph for Mediterranean Climate of Cape Town

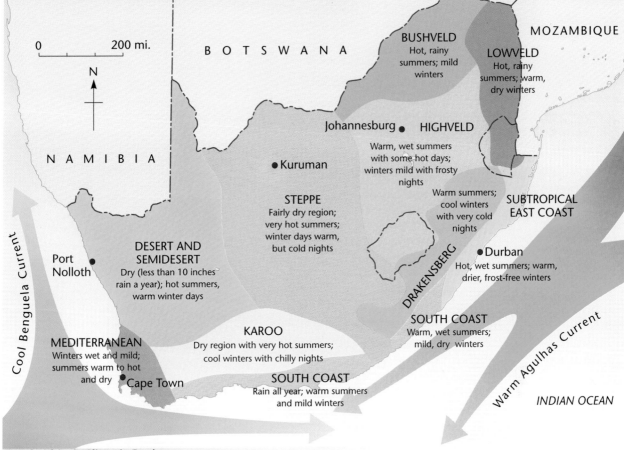

South Africa's Climatic Regions

Kuruman is located in the Northern Cape, close to the border with the North West province. It has an interior location and is cut off from the modifying effect of the oceans. Summers are very hot and winters are very cold.

	J	F	M	A	M	J	J	A	S	O	N	D
Mean temperature (°F)	77	75	70	64	57	50	50	55	62	68	70	73
Precipitation (in.)	3	3.1	3	2	.75	.4	.2	.4	.6	1	1.4	2.2

Total precipitation 18.05 inches
Climate Data for the Interior City of Kuruman

FACT FILE

The effect of ocean currents

South Africa's subtropical location accounts for its warm temperatures. In addition, it falls within the belt of high pressure that generally provides dry conditions. Hence, its average climate is one that is dry and warm. Nevertheless, the oceans on three of its four sides have a moderating effect.

On the east coast the warm Agulhas current raises temperatures, whereas on the west coast the cold Benguela current reduces temperatures. There is a temperature difference of about 42°F between Durban on the east coast and Port Nolloth on the west coast, even though they share the same **latitude**. The east coast areas are warmer and wetter. This is a result of the moister, unstable air over the warm Indian Ocean.

By contrast, over the west coast, air is chilled by the cold Benguela current and largely prevents rain from forming. Port Nolloth receives on average just 2.5 inches of rain a year, compared with 40 inches in Durban.

Rivers, Floods, and Irrigation

> ▶ There are floods in South Africa as well as droughts.
> ▶ Farmers need help to overcome these hazards.

In South Africa, the variable climate causes a number of **natural hazards** that bring damage and destruction.
- Drought is a problem in many areas, especially for farmers.
- South Africa's rivers have great variations in flow at different times of the year; there can be times of not enough flow; there can be times of too much; then there is flooding.

Floods do not occur at the same time throughout the country. For example, in the summer month of December 1995, more than 100 people were killed in flooding caused by heavy rains in KwaZulu-Natal. Most victims were from Imbali, a town near the black township of Edendale. The rains caused the Umsunduze River and its tributary to overflow. People responded in many ways to the floods. Some tried to protect their properties by blocking the doors, while others left

Flash floods swept KwaZulu-Natal in December 1995.

the area. After the floods, some people rebuilt their houses with available material. Others stayed away and moved to other places.

By contrast, the 1994 floods in Cape Town occurred in the winter month of July. Fierce winter storms swept through the area for two weeks, affecting about 20,000 people. The South African government provided a R4,000,000 relief package for flood victims. (R stands for rand, the South Africa monetary unit. R4 million is about 1 million U.S. dollars.) The first to be helped were black residents living in a flooded area east of Cape Town.

Mean Annual **Run-Off** of River Systems

Drainage region	Surface area (sq. mi.)	Annual run-off (million yd³)	Precipitation (inches)	Run-off as % of precipitation
Orange Basin	235,382	13,597	12.25	6.0
West Coast	29,181	1,115	7	0.7
Southwestern Cape	15,787	4,746	19.25	19.9
Southern Cape	33,620	2,282	12	7.2
Southeastern Cape	22,967	1,425	16.5	4.9
Eastern plateau slopes	59,019	25,229	33.25	16.4
Olifants Basin	26,711	3,809	25.75	7.1
Limpopo Main Basin	43,849	3,013	22.5	3.9
Delagoa Bay	17,254	6,584	33	14.8

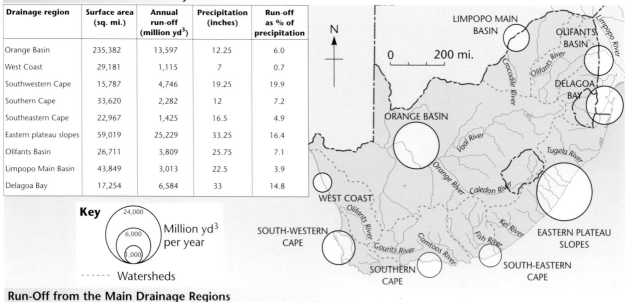

Key
24,000
6,000
1,000
Million yd³ per year
----- Watersheds

Run-Off from the Main Drainage Regions

The government has also been very active in developing irrigation projects, mostly to support white **commercial farms**. By 1982 **irrigation** used 78 percent of all available surface water in South Africa. Government-controlled irrigation plans account for more than 1 million acres, about half of all irrigation in South Africa. Crops grown include citrus fruit, alfalfa, and sugar.

TWO LARGE IRRIGATION PLANS

The Orange River Project is South Africa's largest water development project. It drains an area of 159,000 square miles, with 13.6 percent of South Africa's average run-off. It is designed to improve existing irrigation projects, provide more irrigation in the Lower Orange River Valley, and increase flood protection. The project will also use a 50-mile tunnel to transfer water to the Great Fish River and Sundays River to help meet industrial, domestic, and hydroelectric power (HEP) needs for Port Elizabeth and the Bloemfontein area.

The Lesotho Highlands Water Project is a joint venture with the mountain kingdom of Lesotho. It gives South Africa access to Lesotho's safe and abundant water resources. The Project, agreed to in 1986, has a series of five dams, a power station, 150 miles of tunnels, and two pumping stations. This will also secure water for South Africa's industrial heartland in Gauteng.

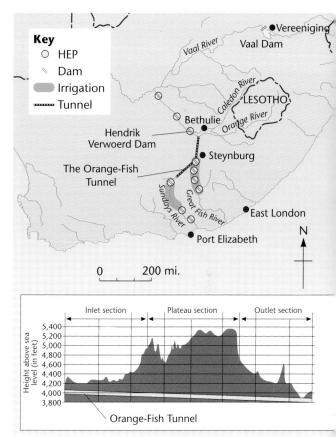

The Orange River Project will irrigate dry farmland.

FACT FILE

Rainfall variability
Rainfall in South Africa is unreliable and unpredictable. Large variations around the mean (average) are the rule rather than the exception. More years have below average rainfall than above average rainfall. In general the higher the rainfall, the less the variation. Hence in the northeast part of the **plateau**, Natal, the east and south coasts have the least variability. By contrast, in the northwest where it is driest, variability is greatest.

Flash floods often occur after long periods of **drought.** Notorious flash floods include those at East London, Eastern Cape, where in 1970 18 inches of rain fell in 24 hours. Similar floods occurred at Port Elizabeth in 1968 and Natal in 1987. The highest rainfall total was recorded in 1984 at Lake St. Lucia when 24 inches of rain fell in just 24 hours.

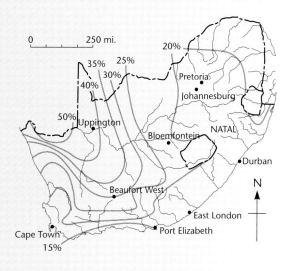

Environmental Issues in South Africa

▶ South Africa has serious environmental problems.
▶ Politics and farming and mining methods are to blame.
▶ History and development are linked to the environmental problems.

South Africa has some of the most serious environmental problems in the world. In both urban and rural areas, the **apartheid** system was mainly to blame. In South Africa the environment is a very political problem.

Environmental problems in rural areas

In the countryside, poor farming methods have led to massive **soil erosion**, and people's need for wood for fuel has led to widespread **deforestation**. The **homelands** were especially at risk with thin topsoil, scarce rainfall, and sloping, rocky ground. Forced resettlements caused overpopulation, leading to more **soil degradation** and deforestation. Under the conditions in which they were forced to live, people had to cut down trees, overuse soil, and pollute streams.

South African farms use many harmful **pesticides** that have been banned in Europe and the U.S., such as DDT. Farm workers often have few rights and cannot read well. They use these poisons with little or no protection in a hot, windy climate.

Industrial pollution clouds the sky near Cape Town.

Environmental problems in urban areas

Conditions in shanty towns and squatter settlements are the most obvious signs of environmental degradation caused by apartheid. Sewage lies in puddles and rotting rubbish chokes alleys and gullies. In the torrential rains of summer, this leads to regular flooding. There is limited electricity, so people burn wood or rubbish. Consequently, a cloud of smoke often covers the **townships**.

During the apartheid years, many oil companies refused to trade with South Africa, so coal is the main source of energy. The low wages paid to black miners keep coal prices low, but as a result coal is used wastefully, worsening pollution.

Mining industries are some of the most damaging to the environment. Mine wastes turn ground and surface waters acid and release **toxic heavy metals**. Smelting metals releases sulphur dioxide and **toxic** air pollutants. Under apartheid, weak environmental controls helped protect South Africa's industries by keeping costs down.

Unprotected, these black workers are exposed to hazardous chemicals.

Disregard for black, colored, and Indian people also led to polluting industries being located on their doorsteps. The Indian township of Merebank, near Durban, is surrounded by two oil refineries, a paper mill, a chromium processing plant, and several smaller chemical factories. Merebank's children are ten times more likely to suffer from respiratory illness than children who live elsewhere.

In the 1970s, concerns about health led mining companies to close down their asbestos mines in Mafefe in the former Northern Transvaal (now Northern Province). But the companies failed to clear the mine waste. Today children play on the dangerous waste heaps between their homes and a nearby river where women fetch water.

Although attitudes towards the environment are beginning to change, it will take years for South Africa's new leaders to repair the damage apartheid has done.

AIR POLLUTION

- Eighty percent of energy comes from coal. Each year this releases
    - one million tons of ash;
    - one million tons of sulphur dioxide;
    - 10,000 tons of iron oxide.
- Factories release 50,000 tons of sulphur dioxide a year.
- Motor vehicles release more than 250 tons of hydrocarbons each year.

Air pollution drifts over a black township. Notice the segmented housing and its nearness to the source of pollution.

FACT FILE

Environmental demands

Only 6 percent of South Africa's land is protected. Another 4 percent is partially protected.

There has been little change in the importance of environmental issues as a national concern since the birth of the "new" South Africa. Such issues are likely to increase in sensitivity as South Africa's population continues to grow, and more and more resources are needed to house, feed, clothe, employ, and provide health care for the rapidly-growing population. Environmental issues could conflict with the demands of future economic growth.

Enviromental issues in South Africa, as in most developed countries, have been seen as a preserve of the rich. This is often in stark contrast to the reality of the impact on the lives of the poor.

"These fields near the sea, these we have always had. But now we are told we can't plant because the place is to be given to the hippopotami."

"Our people do not have tractors to plow the fields. For all our planting we used our hands."

"They have told us to move. We must abandon our fields and our homes and leave behind the graves of our forefathers... They say they want to protect the place. From whom? We have been living here all the time."

"We are made to feel that we are nothing... that animals are better than us."

Source: M. Ramphele, *Restoring the Land*, 1991 (Panos)

Drought and Desertification

▶ Drought and desertification are natural hazards.
▶ These hazards affect people and need to be managed.

We have already seen that South Africa is at risk from a number of **natural hazards**. Some hazards, such as floods, are very obvious. Others, such as **drought** and **desertification**, are more long-term. These natural hazards are made worse by the actions of people, although people can also manage and control them.

Drought is a lack of water caused by high evaporation and low rainfall. About one-third of the world's land is at risk from drought. It is sometimes called a sleeping hazard because it takes a long time to take effect, perhaps over 10 years. Drought has a greater impact in drier areas because it lasts longer and there are fewer reserves of water. In South Africa, drought in the 1980s saw the cattle population decline by 55 percent, while corn yields decreased by 80 per cent in the 1990s.

CORN PRODUCTION

In the 1970s, corn yields varied between 4.2 million tons and 11 million tons. The record year for production was 1980–1981 when 14.2 million tons were produced. Increases in corn production are due to greater use of fertilizer, high-yielding varieties of corn, weed and pest control, and better water conservation in the soil. South Africa needs about seven million tons of corn a year; the rest is **exported.** But during a drought, there is very little surplus available for export.

Desertification is what happens when desert features and processes gradually creep into an area due to climatic changes, such as reduced rainfall. This causes vegetation to die, so more soil is exposed to erosion by wind and water.

A dried-up lake bed is the result of drought.

But **semi-arid** climates are always unpredictable, so some geographers think desertification may not be a long-term problem.

People also cause desertification, or they make it worse. It is often linked to **population pressure**, when more people and their animals use the land. In South Africa, the early 1990s was a time of population growth and forced resettlement into semi-arid areas. This increased the demand for scarce wood for use in cooking, shelter, heating, and fencing. This led to desertification.

It is difficult to stop desertification if its causes are mainly natural. But if it is mainly caused by people, then it is possible to tackle the causes. For example, on a small scale, **check-dams** or **diguettes** can prevent the removal of soil from an area. On a larger scale, the solution may be to reduce population pressure on small areas. Fewer animals would lead to less trampling. Planting trees might reduce wind and water erosion and provide a future source of fuel.

Gully erosion can be caused by **overgrazing.**

Diguettes like this are used to prevent soil erosion.

	1990/1	1991/2	1992/3
Dry beans	100	27	61
Grain sorghum	240	98	380
Peanuts	78	80	119
Soybeans	126	68	60
Sunflower seeds	589	174	364
White corn	3,180	1,232	4,351
Yellow corn	4,016	1,690	4,542

Summer Crop Production (in thousand tons) for 1990/1991–1992/1993

FACT FILE

Elements of desertification

Four elements have been identified in the process of desertification. These are sometimes called the 4 Ds.

- drylands—susceptible to experiencing full desert conditions if mismanaged. This is a climatic definition that implies fragility.

- drought—two or more years with rainfall substantially below the mean average

- degradation—a reduction or destruction of the biological potential. This is usually associated with unsound human practices, such as overgrazing, **deforestation**, trampling, and overproduction.

- desertification—the combination of human and climatic variables which leads to the irreversible decline of the land

Desertification and Soil Erosion in the Eastern Cape

▶ Desertification and soil erosion have natural and human causes.
▶ Improvement is hindered by lack of money to tackle the problem.

Ciskei, one of South Africa's former **homelands**, is now part of the Eastern Cape. It covers a small area (3,000 square miles), but has great contrasts in **relief**, climate, and vegetation. It has four main regions, but only the Amatola Basin is useful for agriculture.

More than 70 percent of the rainfall comes during the summer storms of October and November. On the coast, rainfall is more regular throughout the year. In the north, rainfall amounts are low and irregular. **Drought** in the late 1970s and 1980s made farming even more difficult. In the north, temperature ranges are greater, and there is a greater risk of frost, which shortens the growing season.

Soils in most of the area must be **irrigated** in order to farm. Most of the area has **bushveld** vegetation, suitable only for grazing animals, such as goats. Only one-tenth of the land is suitable for grazing by animals, such as cows.

Land degradation is common in South Africa's former homelands. Up to 46 percent of the land was moderately or severely eroded, and 39 percent of its pastures were **overgrazed**. In Ciskei, half of its surface was more or less eroded. Erosion **gullies** look like small valleys, with many gullies as much as 65 feet deep.

Thornhill was to have been a temporary resettlement camp, one of the many parched, desperately poor communities in the homelands that was artificially created under **apartheid**. Thornhill's population of 660,000 doubled between 1950 and 1980. One-fourth of the population was forcibly relocated here in the 1970s. It is a harsh environment with thousands of brown mud houses and rusty shacks scattered over dry, loose soil. The land cannot sustain the people who live there, and there is little sanitation and water.

Extreme poverty is often closely linked with environmental disasters. With few job opportunities, it is vital for people to plant crops and raise livestock. However, there is not enough land to go around, and the pressure on natural resources increases each year.

In Ciskei, more than half the farms in the best grazing areas are overstocked with cattle by as much as 77 percent. Each household uses three to four tons of wood for fuel per year. In this fragile environment, the vegetation never recovers and **dustbowl** conditions are created.

Soil erosion has also affected water supplies. Many springs have dried up since the 1970s, so much of Ciskei's water is now trucked in. Erosion means the soil absorbs less rainfall, so more water runs off the surface. This causes a downward spiral of environmental and economic crisis. The result is the **migration** of people from the land to the fringes of **urban** areas.

Unfortunately little is being done to improve the environment. The government has little money to tackle the problems. Locally, many young people who could help change things have left, leaving behind an aging population.

LAND USE IN CISKEI

Recommended amount of land for each sheep or goat: 2 acres

Actual amount of land per animal: one-tenth of an acre

	1946	1981
Average size of land holding	4.24 acres	1.1 acres
Landless people	10%	43%

THE IMPACT ON LOCALS

The low rainfall over the past decade devastated agriculture in the area, one resident recalled.

"My three cattle died . . . we had nothing to plow the land . . . we had to wait for the government tractors . . . we had to wait a long time . . . and then the rains did not come."

Dried-up soil is an effect of drought.

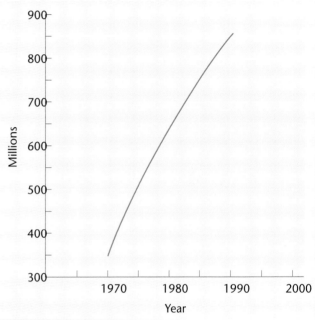

Population Growth in the Eastern Cape, 1970–1990

Even in more watered, fertile areas, overgrazing causes severe soil erosion.

FACT FILE

Soil erosion in the Eastern Cape
The increase in soil erosion is caused by
• climatic change (a more variable/seasonal rainfall)
• vegetation removal (due to increased population pressure)
• cultivation of marginal lands (dry areas)
• intensification of agriculture
• heavier and more powerful machinery
• compaction of soil
• cultivation of steeper slopes
• field enlargement
• hedgerow removal
• planting of winter grains

The impact of soil erosion includes
• declining **productivity**
• decreasing organic and moisture content
• increased turbidity (murkiness) in streams

3 HUMAN ENVIRONMENTS

South Africa's Population

> ▶ South Africa's population is made up of four groups.
> ▶ Population density is uneven.
> ▶ The growth rate is high.

A multicultural population

South Africa's population is about 40 million, made up of four main groups shown in the chart on this page. South Africa's black population are the people who lived in South Africa long before the first white **colony** was set up at the Cape in 1652. There are about 31 million black people from different tribal groups, such as the Zulus and the Xhosa. Tribes originally came from specific places, but they now live in all parts of the country, especially in the **urban**-industrial areas.

The five million white people are mostly descended from English and Dutch **colonists**, as well as German, Italian, and Portuguese settlers. The Afrikaner people are descended from Dutch settlers. They have their own language. There are about one million Asians who mainly live in urban areas. Finally there are also some three million people from mixed backgrounds, who were called *colored* under the **apartheid** system.

One important difference among the groups of this **population composition** is their growth and structure. Another is their quality of life.

Population growth

South Africa's population is growing at a rate of about 2.4 percent a year. By the year 2010, South Africa's population could be between 50 and 60 million. The population is growing because more people are being born than are dying. Better health care means **life expectancy** is increasing and **infant mortality rate** is declining. However, these figures do not reflect the statistics of the individual groups.

A youthful population contributes to growth.

	1970	1995
Black	70.5%	76.3%
White	17.0%	12.7%
Colored	9.6%	8.5%
Asian	2.9%	2.5%
Total (millions)	22,707	41,244

Growth has occured in the black population, while other groups have experienced decline.

Population growth varies for the groups. Black people have the highest population growth rates, nearly 3 percent a year, because of their youthful population. Population growth also varies across the country. Between 1948 and 1990, the most rapid growth was in the black **townships** and the **homelands**. A fast-growing population puts pressure on the environment and resources, as well as on services, such as education and health.

Population distribution

The distribution of South Africa's population is very uneven. There are high **population densities** where resources, industry, and services attract people and help them to make a living. Examples are urban-industrial areas, such as Gauteng, around major cities, such as Durban, and rural areas with good opportunities for farming.

In general, population decreases from the southeast to northwest. This partly reflects the distribution of rainfall in South Africa. The lowest densities are found in the most arid areas and also in parts of the mountains. **Population distribution** is also changing. After the end of apartheid, thousands of people left the homelands and **migrated** to large cities in search of employment.

	1960	1990	1994
Life expectancy			
Men	55.7 years	60.7 years	60 years
Women	59.7 years	66.3 years	75 years
Infant Mortality (per 1000 births)	80	62	53
Fertility (average number of children a woman has)	6	4.6	4

Improved health care causes changes in life expectancy, infant mortality, and fertility rates.

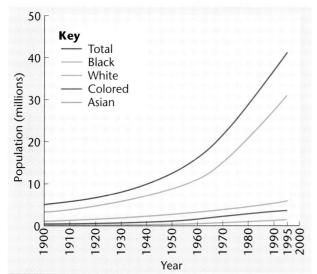

Population Growth in South Africa, 1900–2000

Key
— Total
— Black
— White
— Colored
— Asian

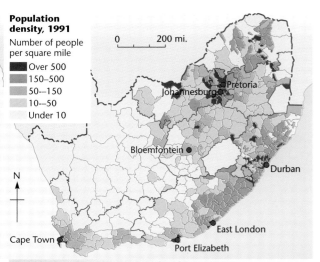

Population density, 1991
Number of people per square mile
■ Over 500
150–500
50–150
10–50
Under 10

Population Density in South Africa, 1991

FACT FILE

South Africa's population
South Africa's main racial groups—1998 estimate

	Million	**%**
Black	31.5	76
White	5.4	13
Asian	1.2	3
Colored	3.3	8
Total	41.4	100

Racial diversity is reflected by a diversity in languages. South Africa has 11 official languages.

Official language	**Percent of population**
Zulu	22.4
Xhosa	18.3
Afrikaans	14.5
Pedi	9.1
English	8.4
Setswana	7.7
Sesotho	6.4
Tsonga	3.7
Siswati	3.1
Venda	1.7
Ndebele	0.7
Other languages	4.0

Population Change

Population changes are due to
- changes in the **birth rate**—the number of children born
- changes in the **death rate**—the number of people dying
- **migration**—people moving into or out of the country

The difference between the birth and death rates is called the rate of **natural increase**. Because the birth rate in South Africa is much higher than the death rate, the population is growing fast. The balance of birth and death rates is a good sign of a country's development, because they are linked with people's health, wealth, and education. In South Africa, the differences between black and white people clearly show the inequalities brought about under **apartheid**.

The birth rate
What causes high birth rates? People want children
- to help out and earn money
- to look after them in old age
- to replace other children who have died
- to continue the family name
- for status

The **infant mortality rate (IMR)** is still very high. It is one of the reasons that the birth rate is also high.

Birth rates decline when
- women are well-educated
- women can make choices about their lives and work
- the government looks after people through pensions and health services
- family planning services are available
- infant mortality is low, because then there is less need to replace children
- children are expensive to raise

The death rate
High death rates are caused by
- a lack of clean water
- poor hygiene and sanitation
- lack of food
- overcrowding and disease
- poverty

Death rates decline when there is
- clean water and good hygiene and sanitation
- a reliable food supply
- lower **population densities**
- better health care
- rising standards of living

	1970	1980	1990
Black*			
Birth rate	40.0	40.0	35.0
Death rate	12.0	12.0	12.0
White			
Birth rate	22.9	16.5	13.8
Death rate	8.9	8.3	6.6
Colored			
Birth rate	34.1	27.1	23.8
Death rate	13.3	8.8	7.6
Asian			
Birth rate	32.3	24.1	20.6
Death rate	6.7	5.9	4.3

* estimates
Changes in Birth and Death Rates, 1970–1990

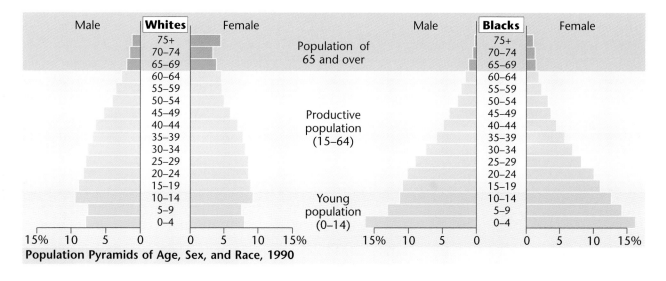

Population Pyramids of Age, Sex, and Race, 1990

Age	0–4	5–9	10–14	15–19	20–24	25–29	30–34	35–39	40–44	45–49	50–54	55–59	60–64	65–69	70–74	75+
Male %	10.0	10.5	11.5	10.5	10.0	9.0	8.5	8.0	5.5	5.0	4.0	3.0	2.0	1.5	1.0	1.0
Female %	10.0	10.5	11.5	10.5	10.0	9.0	8.5	8.0	5.5	5.0	3.5	2.5	2.0	2.0	0.5	2.0

Population Structure: South African People

Population structure
Population pyramids show the balance between males and females and the balance between different age groups. In South Africa, population pyramids also compare and contrast the different groups. The pyramid for black people shows a high proportion of children because birth rates are high. The pyramid for white people has fewer children and more people over the age of 65, due to a lower birth rate and longer life expectancy.

FACT FILE

The Demographic Transition Model (DTM)
The DTM describes how birth rates and death rates change over time. It is divided into four stages (and sometimes a fifth).
Stage 1 Early expanding
- birth rates and death rates are high and variable
- population growth fluctuates
- there are no countries now at this stage, except for some indigenous (primitive) tribes

Stage 2 Early expanding
- birth rate remains high, but the death rate declines rapidly
- population growth is rapid
- countries such as Afghanistan, Sudan, and Libya are at this stage

Stage 3 Late expanding
- birth rate declines, death rate remains low
- population growth continues, but at a smaller rate
- Brazil and Argentina are at this stage

Stage 4 Low and variable
- birth rates and death rates are low and variable
- population growth fluctuates
- most developed countries are now at this stage

Stage 5 Low and declining
- birth rate is lower than the death rate
- the population declines

Measuring Development in South Africa

▶ The Human Development Index includes three measures of a good life.
▶ The Human Development Index varies within South Africa.

Many black South Africans have a very low standard of living.

Municipal, or council, housing is provided for this family in Dimbaza, Eastern Cape.

The Human Development Index (HDI) is used by the United Nations to measure human development. It includes three measures of a decent life.
• Life expectancy
• Knowledge (**adult literacy** and average number of years in school)
• Standard of living, adjusted to the local cost of living

The HDI can help show differences between countries. In general, wealthier countries with a high **gross national product (GNP)** also have a high HDI. But these national averages can hide differences within a country, for example between the racial groups in South Africa.

The map on the next page shows development variations between South Africa's regions. South Africa's least developed areas are the former **homelands**, where most people are poorly-paid farm workers. By contrast, high HDIs are found near major cities, on the KwaZulu-Natal coastline, and along parts of the Garden Route, the coastal area between Cape Town and George. These are rich, fertile areas that attract wealthy people and create productive agriculture.

Rank	Country	HDI rating	GNP($ US) per person (1994)
1	Canada	0.932	20,520
16	U.K.	0.911	17,160
23	Spain	0.888	13,400
	White South Africans	0.878	N/A
24	Hong Kong	0.875	20,340
54	Thailand	0.798	8,950
93	**South Africa**	0.650	3,799
94	China	0.644	1,950
122	Cape Verde	0.474	1,750
	Black South Africans	0.462	N/A
123	Congo	0.461	2,870
173	Guinea	0.191	592

United Nations Human Development Index, 1994

South Africa has huge inequalities in wealth and standard of living. Up to 16 million people live below the **Minimum Living Level**. This includes 33 percent of black households in **urban** areas, and 80 percent in rural areas. By contrast, 38 percent of South Africa's white people earn between R10,000 ($2,500) and R29,999 ($7,500).

Infant mortality rate

The **infant mortality rate (IMR)** shows the number of children (of every 1,000 born) who die before their first birthday. It is a good indicator of a nation's development, because babies' health is affected by water supply, sanitation, housing, food supply, and income levels. The lower the IMR the more developed the country. In South Africa, IMR rates are declining as the country develops. But there are big differences in IMR between rural and urban areas, and between different groups.

FACT FILE

The infant mortality rate
In South Africa, reliable statistics relating to the IMR are scarce, although it is possible to see the main trends.
• First, it varies with race, whites have lower rates (about 10–15 percent) than blacks (about 50–100 percent). Although the rates for both are decreasing. The latest data suggest rates per thousand of more than 52 for blacks, 28 for coloreds, 13.5 for Indians, and 7.3 for whites.
• The IMR also varies spatially, being higher in the **peri-urban** and rural areas compared with urban areas. Nevertheless, there is considerable variation between cities, as well as within cities, ranging from 12 percent in Durban to 41.3 percent in Port Elizabeth.
Cause and time of death for infants also varies.
• For whites, **neonatal** and **perinatal** deaths were more likely due to congenital deformities.
• By contrast black deaths are more likely to be due to low birth-weight, gastroenteritis, pneumonia, and jaundice, occurring between 7 and 365 days, the post-neonatal period.

Human Development, 1993

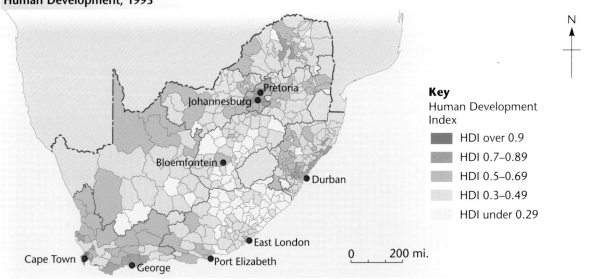

Key
Human Development Index
■ HDI over 0.9
■ HDI 0.7–0.89
■ HDI 0.5–0.69
■ HDI 0.3–0.49
□ HDI under 0.29

	Black	White	Colored	Indian
Infant mortality rate (per 1,000 live births)	52.8	7.3	28.0	3.5
Life expectancy (years)	63	73	63	67
TB cases per 100,000 people	216	15	580	53
School expenditure per head (rand)	1,248	4,448	2,701	3,500
School pass rate (%)	41	96	83	95
Average monthly income (rand)	779	4,679	1,607	2,476

Social and Economic Indicators in South Africa, 1993

Migration in South Africa

▶ Migration is the movement of people.
▶ Different types of migration have occurred in South Africa.

Migration is the movement of people from one place to another. It is a permanent change in the place a person lives. Migration generally occurs over a long distance, rather than small-scale movements within a town or city. Migration can be forced or voluntary.

South Africa has had three main periods of migration in the twentieth century.
- economic migration linked with industrial development until 1950
- forced migration related to apartheid
- voluntary migration following the collapse of the **apartheid** system

Industry in South Africa developed rapidly between the two world wars. Many black people migrated from the rural areas to the cities to work in the growing gold and diamond mines. As the population grew in the cities, there was increased demand for food products. Agricultural Marketing Boards guaranteed farmers a fixed price for their goods, which made farming profitable. Many farmers evicted black tenants from their land. These people returned to the **reserves** (early forms of **homelands**) or the **townships**.

Between 1948 and 1994 the white National Party had political control of South Africa and set up the apartheid policy. Under this policy, over four million black people were forcibly removed from "white" areas and relocated to the homelands. At the same time, there were severe restrictions on black people entering "white" towns. These restrictions were known as **influx control**. Industries and farms owned by white people were able to recruit black workers from the homelands.

Since the end of apartheid, many black people have migrated from the homelands in search of work in large cities. However, because of poverty, they are forced to live in the townships on the edge of cities. So although apartheid is officially over, for many people **discrimination** is still widespread due to poverty.

There is also much migration among the white population. In the first part of this century, many white people were **immigrants** from Europe. Since 1990, over 250,000 white people have **emigrated** from South Africa. Also, a small number of Afrikaners have left South Africa and set up farms in neighboring countries.

Migration in South Africa, 1935–1950

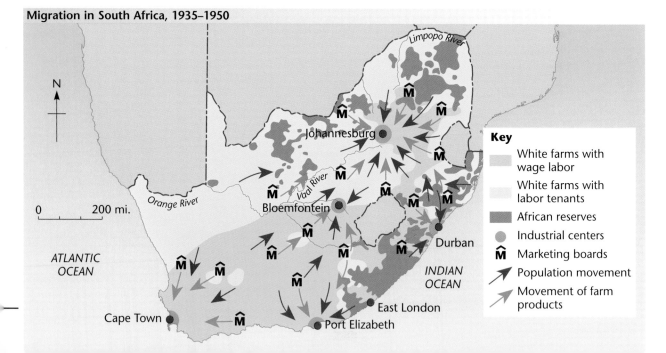

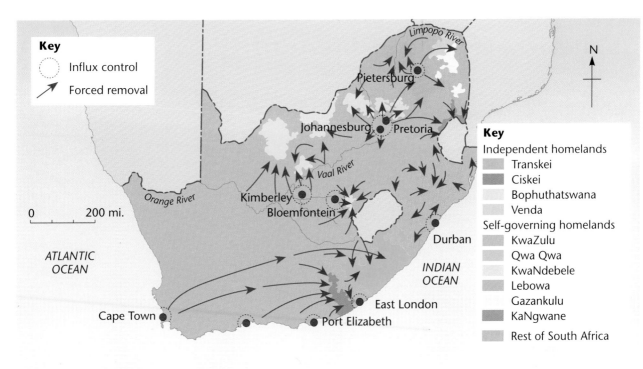

Key

- ⊙ Influx control
- ↗ Forced removal

Key

Independent homelands
- Transkei
- Ciskei
- Bophuthatswana
- Venda

Self-governing homelands
- KwaZulu
- Qwa Qwa
- KwaNdebele
- Lebowa
- Gazankulu
- KaNgwane
- Rest of South Africa

Migration in South Africa, 1960–1990

FORCED REMOVALS TO DIMBAZA, CISKEI

Dimbaza is a dumping ground for the unwanted and nonproductive population. They were dumped in isolated settlements lacking all services. They were the poorest, the least skilled, the least organized groups of people in South Africa.

—a local priest

In Uppingham we thought we were third-class citizens. When we were driven to Dimbaza, we realized we were not citizens at all, and we didn't have any class either. We were moved about just like cattle being taken to market.

—a resident removed to Dimbaza

FACT FILE

Migration

South Africa's long history of migration is shown in the map key and the map below.

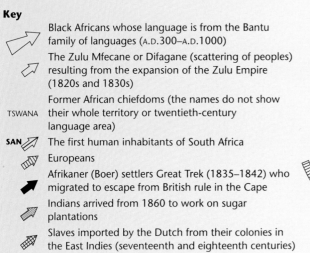

Key

- ⇨ Black Africans whose language is from the Bantu family of languages (A.D.300–A.D.1000)
- ⇨ The Zulu Mfecane or Difagane (scattering of peoples) resulting from the expansion of the Zulu Empire (1820s and 1830s)
- TSWANA Former African chiefdoms (the names do not show their whole territory or twentieth-century language area)
- SAN ↗ The first human inhabitants of South Africa
- ⇗ Europeans
- ➤ Afrikaner (Boer) settlers Great Trek (1835–1842) who migrated to escape from British rule in the Cape
- ⇗ Indians arrived from 1860 to work on sugar plantations
- ⇗ Slaves imported by the Dutch from their colonies in the East Indies (seventeenth and eighteenth centuries)

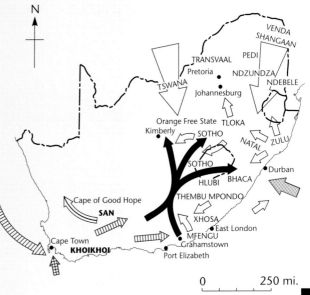

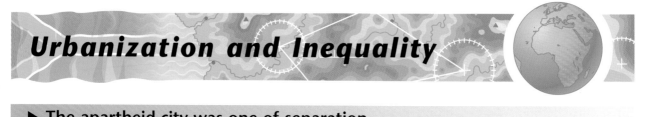
▶ The apartheid city was one of separation.
▶ The law no longer supports segregation.

Urbanization

South Africa's **urban** areas are increasing at a tremendous rate. In 1990, 63 percent of South Africa's population were urbanized, ranging from 89 percent among white, colored, and Indian people to 50 percent among black people. By 2000, 33 million people (75 percent) will live in urban areas.

Now that the restrictions of **apartheid** have been removed, black **urbanization** is rising rapidly. Up to fourteen million more black people will live in urban areas over the next two decades. How will this affect the **post-apartheid city** in South Africa?

An aerial view shows Kayelitsha township, Cape Town.

The apartheid city was planned with a special layout.

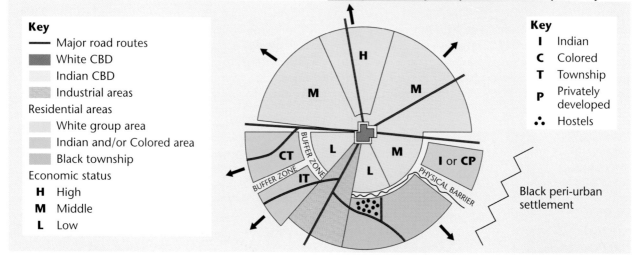

Key
— Major road routes
White CBD
Indian CBD
Industrial areas
Residential areas
White group area
Indian and/or Colored area
Black township
Economic status
H High
M Middle
L Low

Key
I Indian
C Colored
T Township
P Privately developed
∴ Hostels

Black peri-urban settlement

The apartheid city

Cities in South Africa were planned cities. In the center was the central business district (CBD), which was predominately white people. This CBD was surrounded by white residential areas. Colored, Indian, and black **townships** were separated from the white areas by physical barriers, parks, or industrial zones.

The post-apartheid city

After apartheid, one change has been that groups are not segregated into different areas by law. But the biggest problem is the speed of urbanization.

Apartheid is no longer the law.

The urban population is growing rapidly as a result of **migration** and **natural increase**, especially in squatter settlements. There are serious difficulties in providing even the basic necessities of life, such as water and sanitation, as well as providing health care, education, and employment.

But in the future, the structure of cities is unlikely to change much unless resources, wealth, and opportunities are shared more equally. Few black people will be able to afford houses in the former white areas, especially the more expensive areas. Most white people will not want to live in the townships.

Not everyone has adequate housing in Eastern Cape.

Many black people will still live in squatter shacks in the sprawling **peri-urban** townships, without adequate water, sanitation, or jobs. Most people with jobs will continue to face long and expensive journeys to work in the city.

The housing crisis

South Africa faces some of the worst housing problems in the world, and the backlog of over one million houses is rising rapidly. New housing generally favors whites. In 1991 only one-fourth of new houses were built at a cost of less than R65,000 ($16,250), so new houses are built for the wealthy, more of whom are white. Since most black people earn less than R2,000 ($500) a month, their chance of buying a new home is limited.

Informal, or squatter, housing in Eastern Cape is not a solution.

Improving housing is a top priority for the new government, but there is a severe shortage of funds. Building starter homes may be one solution. Each house has a core foundation, one room, and basic services for a cost of about R20,000 ($5,000). These can be upgraded when the occupant can afford it.

THE HOUSING CRISIS

- 13 million people without adequate housing
- 4.4 million households set up in 3.4 million homes
- 4.5 million squatter houses
- 35 percent of squatter houses are in cities, 65 percent are in rural areas
- 33 percent of the rural population live in adequate housing
- average floor area is 355 sq. ft. per white person, 43 sq. ft. per black person

FACT FILE

Urban inequality

Fly into any South African city and the divisions are precise and entrenched. Johannesburg offers the most vivid example. On one side, there is Sandton municipality, where, in fortified splendor, live some of the most pampered people on Earth. They do not all live in Italianate palaces with decorative fountains rising out of decorative lawns.

. . . But white enclaves, such as Sandton, are apartheid's unchallenged bastions, from which 5 percent of the population control 88 percent of the nation's wealth. This grotesque imbalance of power has not changed since democracy.

Source: *The Guardian*, April 11, 1998

Rural Settlement

▶ Rural areas are predominately substandard.
▶ The village of Welcome Wood was developed to house black people.
▶ The study of remote areas is aided by aerial photography.

In rural areas, only 33 percent of the population has decent quality houses. Up to ten million people live in informal, or squatter, houses that are substandard huts and shacks made of available materials. These houses are often overcrowded, with as many as eleven people per house who have little access to facilities like water, sanitation, and electricity.

Welcome Wood is a rural area in the Eastern Cape and Border region of South Africa. Parts of the area were originally used for **commercial farming**, but much of the land is too hilly and steep for farming. The village of Welcome Wood was developed in order to house black people displaced by the **apartheid** system. It is a village of about 2,000 people with a primary school, clinic, and two water taps.

A photograph of the main road in Welcome Wood shows the day-care center (white building), the school, and the clinic.

An aerial photograph, looking south from Welcome Wood towards the Indian Ocean, shows the vegetation, slopes, and landforms of the area.

FACT FILE

Maps and orthophotos
Maps tell a great deal about the landscape and the activities that take place in an area, and photographs can help tell about a place and give a feeling for what a place is like. Geographers use many tools in their attempts to understand people and places. The three methods here—surveys, aerial photography, and photographs—give a feeling for a place that is many thousands of miles away.

An aerial photograph with elevation contour lines gives a visual impression of an area and provides data about the **relief** of an area. Aerial photgraphs are often used for remote areas where it is easier to send in photographers in airplanes, rather than engineers on the ground. They are a quick and efficient way of learning about an area.

In remote areas, as well as rapidly changing areas, such as South Africa's **townships**, the use of aerial photographs and satellites are essential for geographers to map an area and assess levels of change. Population census occurs only every ten years or so. This makes aerial photos a great help in the years between censuses to estimate the physical and human geography of an area.

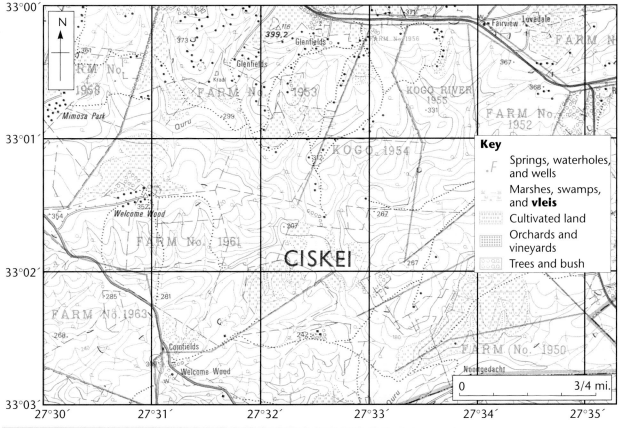

Survey Map of Welcome Wood

Key

.F Springs, waterholes, and wells

Marshes, swamps, and **vleis**

Cultivated land

Orchards and vineyards

Trees and bush

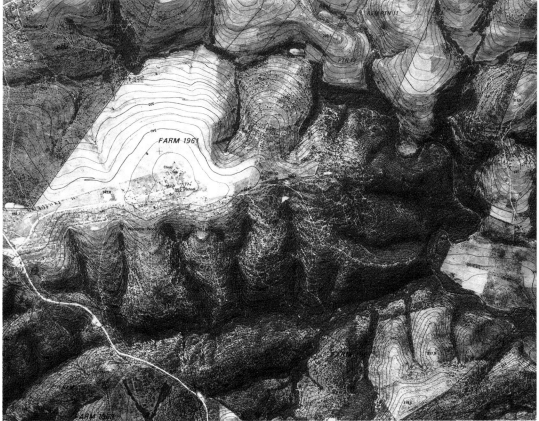

This aerial photograph with contour lines helps in the study of Welcome Wood.

A Black Township, Fingo Village, Grahamstown

▶ **Fingo Village has economic, social, and environmental problems.**
▶ **The area has been affected by changing population and inequality.**

Conditions are harsh in Fingo Village, Grahamstown.

Environmental quality is low in Fingo Village.

- low household incomes, most less than R500 ($125) per month
- many people traveling long distances to work, often two to three hours each day
- many of the very poor people spending up to 70 percent of their income on food, 10 percent on fuel, and up to 10 percent on rent and transportation; they have very little money to spend on luxuries

There are also many related social problems.
- more than 50 percent of the population is under 18 years old
- large households, on average more than six people per household
- rapid population growth, as much as 4 percent per year
- many illnesses such as tuberculosis, measles, diarrhea, and vomiting
- very high rates of crime
- lack of adequate schools and health care

There are also many environmental problems.
- poor quality housing without services such as electricity, sanitation, and running water
- poor roads and communications
- widespread and increasing air, water, and soil pollution

Fingo Village is a black **township** on the outskirts of Grahamstown in the Eastern Cape. Conditions in the whole of this region are poor, but they are very harsh in some townships like Grahamstown. There are a number of economic, social, and environmental problems.

There are serious economic problems.
- 34 percent unemployment
- 28 percent underemployment (people with jobs who would like to work longer hours)
- high rents for housing
- low wages, with average weekly wages of R100 ($25)

A FINGO VILLAGE RESIDENT WHO WORKS AT RHODES UNIVERSITY

In some ways we are lucky. There are jobs at Rhodes University although they are not very well paid. Our houses are OK—but compared with the ones in parts of Grahamstown, such as Cross Street, they are small, overcrowded, and lacking in facilities. We could be worse off—we certainly could be better off. Personally I get very tired having to walk up the hill to Rhodes each day. But at least it's a job. It means I can support my family. I wish that Fingo Village had more play areas, a sports ground for instance. Perhaps Nelson Mandela will be able to work it out.

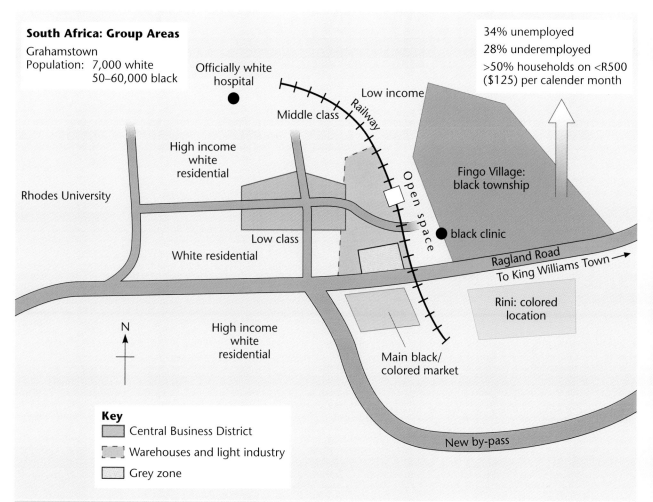

South Africa: Group Areas

Grahamstown
Population: 7,000 white
50–60,000 black

34% unemployed
28% underemployed
>50% households on <R500 ($125) per calender month

Officially white hospital

Low income

Middle class

Railway

High income white residential

Fingo Village: black township

Rhodes University

Open space

black clinic

Low class
White residential

Ragland Road
To King Williams Town →

N

High income white residential

Rini: colored location

Main black/ colored market

Key
- Central Business District
- Warehouses and light industry
- Grey zone

New by-pass

Fingo Village, Grahamstown, mapped out like this during the apartheid era.

FACT FILE

Housing inequality

Housing inequality is the most concrete illustration of the legacy of **apartheid**. Whereas most white South Africans live in adequately serviced and comfortable housing, the majority of black South Africans live in overcrowded dwellings that often lack basic services.

Countrywide, about 13 million people do not have adequate housing. In 1990 it was estimated that 60 percent of the 1.8 million African people residing in the Durban area lived in shacks, and in Gauteng, half of its African population, about 2.6 million people, resided in backyard or free-standing shacks. Seventy percent, about 5.7 million, of South African households earn less than R1,500 ($375) a month and do not have

the financial means to acquire a home of their own.

The backlog of housing is one of many problems that the South African government is having to face. There are related problems of education, health, welfare, and economic development. The government would like private companies to provide housing, rather than have the government pay for them all. However, private companies want to make a profit. So they build houses for the rich and not for the poor. This causes a lack of affordable housing in South Africa.

4 ECONOMIC ENVIRONMENTS

The Two Sides of South African Agriculture

▶ Two types of farming are found in South Africa.
▶ Black and white farmers have different farming experiences.
▶ Farmers face a shortage of land, a growing population, and poverty.

South Africa's agriculture shows the two sides of the country's economy. The contrasts between the mainly white **commercial farms** and the mainly black **subsistence farms** are great. Commercial farms produce 90 percent of the income from farming, but most jobs are in subsistence black farming.

In some ways farming is a success story. In normal years, South Africa produces good food surpluses, and 30 percent of exports apart from gold come from agricultural products. South Africa produces
- more than 50 percent of the food for Southern Africa
- 45 percent of Africa's corn and wool production
- 27 percent of Africa's wheat
- 20 percent of Africa's potatoes
- 17 percent of Africa's red meat

Commercial agriculture
Commercial agriculture in South Africa is dominated by white farmers, although their numbers are decreasing. For example, in the 1950s there were more than 100,000 commercial farmers, but by 1995, there were only 65,000. The development of commercial agriculture has been based on exploiting the black labor force.

Farming in the former homelands
Although the black **homelands** no longer exist, little has changed there. Partly due to the variety of the natural environments, black agriculture varies greatly, too. In 1955 a government report found that the homeland areas had up to 50 percent more good farmland

than areas in white South Africa. However, this did not take into account the problems of **accessibility** and **population pressure**.

The problems of black subsistence agriculture are linked to a shortage of land, a growing population, and increasing poverty. These lead to
- overcrowding
- overgrazing
- use of poor land
- soil erosion
- declining yields

White commercial farming is on the decline.

Black subsistence farming is plagued with problems.

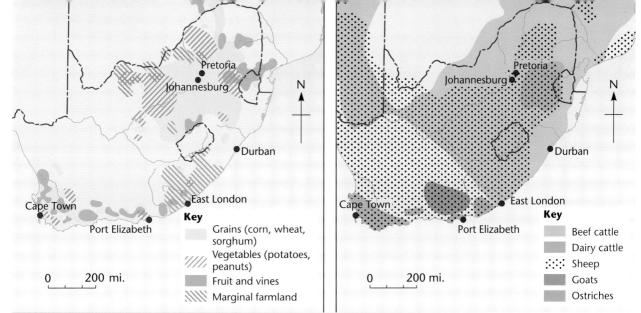

Commercial Agriculture in South Africa

Map keys:

Key (left map)
- Grains (corn, wheat, sorghum)
- Vegetables (potatoes, peanuts)
- Fruit and vines
- Marginal farmland

Key (right map)
- Beef cattle
- Dairy cattle
- Sheep
- Goats
- Ostriches

	Homeland area (mostly black)	Non-homeland area (mostly white)	Total
Total area (million acres)	42.7	252.6	259.3
Farmland (acre)	39.8	205.2	244.9
Rural population (million)	13.1	5.3	18.4
Farmland per person (acre)	0.5	38.8	13.3
Average farm size (acre)	2.5	3,210	

	Homeland area (mostly black)	Non-homeland area (mostly white)
Share of marketed production	4%	96%
Average productivity per person per year	R5/acre	R27.16/acre
Share of agricultural GDP	10%	90%

The tables show the inequalities found in South African farming in 1990.

FACT FILE

Black agriculture

Working conditions for blacks vary greatly. For most, wages are very low, and there is limited security. Wages are frequently only about 10 percent of manufacturing wages although **payment in kind** sometimes doubles their income. At one extreme there are farms where flogging, child labor, and payment by the "tot" system (part payment in the form of alcohol) is common. Weekly wages can be as low as R35 ($8.75) for women and R45 ($11.25) for men. At the other extreme, some farmers provide their laborers with three-bedroom houses, day care facilities, a school, and a library. Wages of up to R125 ($31.25) per week were reported.

Some of the best farmland in South Africa is in homeland areas, namely KwaZulu and Transkei. By contrast, homeland also has some of the worst farmland, such as in Ciskei. In a recent survey of

	1970	1980	1990	2000	2020
Cultivated	1.5	1.2	1.0	0.75	0.5
Other	13.6	10.4	7.9	5.9	3.7

Acres per Person in South Africa, 1970–2020

homeland areas, 31 percent of rural households were living below subsistence levels, 13 percent of rural households farmed on a small scale, and only 0.2 percent of farmers farmed on a commercial basis.

Total food production in the homeland areas is sufficient for about one-third of the homeland needs. The failure to modernize and to increase output is related to a number of factors.
- limited size of plots
- yields up to five times less than on white farms
- up to 20 to 30 percent of the land left unused

Manufacturing and Economic Change

▶ South Africa is an important industrial country.
▶ Big business faces some big problems.
▶ The informal economy is vibrant.

South Africa's resources

The South African economy is the largest in the whole of the African continent, although its future is very uncertain. South Africa's strength lies in its resources. In human resources, South Africa has a large established workforce and an **infrastructure** (factories, mines, roads, transportation networks) that was built over many years of industrial growth.

Manganese	79%
Platinum	70%
Chromium	55%
Gold	48%
Alumino-silicates	38%
Vanadium	33%

South Africa produces large percentages of some of the world's mineral resources.

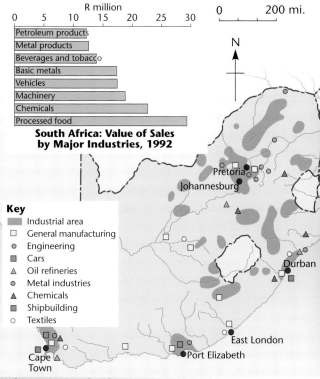

South Africa: Value of Sales by Major Industries, 1992

Industry in South Africa

Jobs and incomes

About one-third of the population is employed. Most are in manufacturing industry (19 percent) and government (17 percent). In most jobs, differences in wages between black and white workers have declined over the last twenty years, but there is still a big difference in overall incomes.

The **formal economy** does not provide enough job opportunities for the majority of the population, but there is a vibrant **informal economy**. This includes a variety of jobs such as domestic work, gardening, selling food, taxi driving, and operating shebeens (illegal drinking parlors). Black businesses are held back by a lack of credit from banks; poor training and skills; violence, theft, and instability in **townships**; and competition from white and overseas businesses.

	Agriculture	Industry	Services
1970	21%	22%	57%
1994	13%	25%	62%

Indicator of Change in the Economy: Jobs

Monthly Household Income, 1993	
Black	R662
Colored	R1,279
Indian	R2,005
White	R3,931

Share of Personal Income, 1993		
	% of population	Share of income
Black	74%	33%
White	14%	54%

Incomes have improved, but differences remain.

South Africa's problems

South Africa's economy is uncompetitive. For example, it costs more to transport steel from the center of South Africa to Durban than it does to transport it from Durban to Europe. Many South African industries survived in the past only because of state protection and subsidies. Today some companies serve very small markets and therefore have high costs. Although labor in South Africa is inexpensive, the **productivity** is very low. South Africa is not as rich as it seems. Its **gross domestic product (GDP)** per capita, a measurement of its wealth, is similar to Brazil's or Botswana's.

A major problem facing the new government is that economic growth is only 1 percent a year, while population growth is 3 percent. Since 1991 new investment has been limited. The reasons include uncertainty about South African's future, continuing violence, high rates of inflation, and increased competition from other developing countries.

FACT FILE

The need for economic changes
South Africa needs an economic transformation just as far-reaching as that achieved in the political arena. Its new government has to reach growth rates comparable to the Asian **newly industrized countries (NIC)** if it is to redress the legacy of **apartheid**.

South Africa needs higher productivity, more flexible labor markets, and more efficient management if it is to become internationally competitive. Although it has received overseas investment, many investors are reluctant to invest too much.

One area of growth has been in the taxi service. This has developed into a powerful feature of the urban informal economy. The 10 to 15-seater minibus taxis are faster and more flexible than buses and trains, so they are very popular. However they are often overcrowded, and they charge high fares. As they are often driven recklessly, accidents are frequent. Despite this, the staggering growth of taxis has been an important part in the development of small businesses by black people in South Africa.

South Africa's black taxis are one of the most vibrant parts of the informal ecomomy.

South Africa is uncompetitive. The following figures show labor costs and manpower hours needed to construct a car in South Africa, Mexico, and the U.S.

	Labor costs per hour	Labor hours per car	Labor costs per car
South Africa	$ 5.60	64	$358.40
Mexico	$ 6.00	24	$144.00
U.S.	$38.00	19	$722.00

Gold Mining: An Industry under Threat

▶ **Gold is important to South Africa.**
▶ **The decline of gold prices has an effect on the economy and people.**

Gold has been an important part of the economy since the 1880s. Gold allowed South Africa to change from an economy based mainly on agriculture to one based on mining. Some of the profits from gold and diamond mining were invested in manufacturing industries. This broadened and strengthened the economy.

Problems in gold mining

Gold is an important **resource** and **raw material**. However, the future of gold mining is not healthy and production is falling. There are two main problems.

• The world price of gold is falling, reaching a twelve-year low in 1997. At this price, more than half of South Africa's gold mines are unprofitable. If prices do not recover, as many as 50,000 jobs could be lost.

• South Africa has among the highest mining costs in the world compared with foreign competitors. This is due to gold deposits that are deep underground and a lack of mechanization because of a reliance on inexpensive labor.

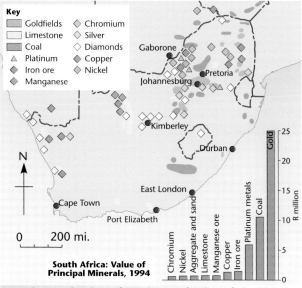

Location and Value of Mining and Minerals in 1994

Effects on the economy and people

South Africa's gold production accounts for about 25 percent of **gross domestic product (GDP)** and over 50 percent of export earnings. Any fall in output and export earnings will negatively affect the country.

As the price of gold falls, mining companies and workers are faced with the threat of mines

Date	Production (tons)	Value (thousands rand)
1920	253	91,212
1930	333	91,040
1940	436	235,981
1950	361	289,552
1960	665	536,019
1970	1,000	831,233
1980	672	10,369,275
1986	638	17,283,251
1996	300	5,650,432

Gold Production in South Africa from 1920 to 1996

Supply of gold	Tons	%	Marketing	Demand for gold	Tons	%
Production						
South Africa	621	40.4	Price $437	Jewelry	1,484	80.2
U.S. and Canada	334	21.7		Electronics and dentistry	183	9.9
Other	583	37.9		Other industrial uses	59	3.2
Total production	1,538	100.0		Medals and official coins	118	6.4
Recycled gold	258			Investment	6	0.3
Total world supply	2,120		1,850 tons	Total	1,850	100.0

Gold Production, Marketing, and Use for 1988

closing, unemployment, and the decline of communities. For example, the Benoni Plant near Johannesburg closed down in July 1997. At its peak it employed 18,000 people. By 1997 it had fewer than 2,000 workers.

Communities in many parts of the country depend totally on mining for their livelihood. The economic and social effects of mine closure will be felt most in rural areas where mines are often the only source of income. If the mines closed, places like Orkney in the North West and Virginia in the Free State would become ghost towns, and restaurants and shops would be forced to close.

It is not only gold miners whose jobs are at risk. For every three miners, there is at least one other person working in a dependent industry, such as explosives, steel, drilling machinery, and engineering. Also, with more than one-third of the population unemployed, every worker supports on average between seven and ten dependents. So any fall in employment in the mines will have a drastic effect on the economy and on the ability of the government to provide for its citizens.

The misfortunes of the gold mining industry are also felt in other countries. Many **migrant workers** from Lesotho, Swaziland, Zimbabwe, and Mozambique have lost their jobs in the South African mines. These workers contributed up to 70 percent of rural household earnings in their home countries, and they have little prospect of finding new jobs.

Work in a gold mine is uncomfortable, difficult, and dangerous. Above all, employment is uncertain.

FACT FILE

Gold mining—closures and disease

The price of gold has fallen rapidly. Between 1995 and 1998 the price has fallen by more than 33 percent to reach an all-time low. For South African companies, it has been a disaster. JCI, the first black-controlled mining group, was liquidated (closed for business) in April 1998.

Gold price

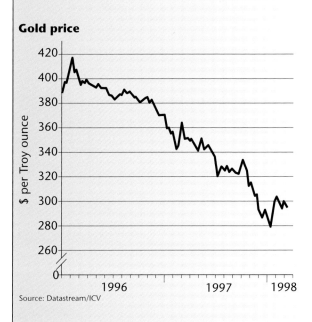

Source: Datastream/ICV

The mining industry has long been associated with diseases such as tuberculosis (TB). TB was not found in South Africa until the development of mining in the late nineteenth century. The mining authorities were able to exploit blacks as a source of inexpensive labor since there was little land available to blacks and new taxes were placed on black farmers.

One reason why TB became such a common illness among the laborers was that they were forced to live in huge compounds—massive single-sex hostels with thousands of workers living in overcrowded conditions. The diet was monotonous—porridge and some meat and beef, and the working day and working conditions were poor. Work shifts of 10–12 hours were common. As the photo to the left shows, the work was very tiring, and done in hot, damp conditions.

TB later spread from the mines to the rural **homelands** as returning migrant workers carried the disease with them.

▶ Energy is important in South Africa.
▶ The government is working to overcome its lack of energy resources.

South Africa's energy problems are a problem for families and for the country as a whole.

Energy for families

For many black families, especially in rural areas, the problem is access to any type of energy. When the Nelson Mandela government took over in 1994, about 3.6 million households, 19,000 black schools, and 2,000 clinics had no electricity. The government is working hard to correct the situation, but it will take years to electrify the whole country.

Meanwhile, each family uses an average of three to four tons of wood a year in a never-ending search for fuel. With this kind of high use, the vegetation does not recover in South Africa's fragile environment. The result is **dustbowl** conditions and **desertification**.

Energy for the country

South Africa has good supplies of coal, some good sites for **hydroelectric power (HEP)**, but no oil supplies. Also, much of the coal is soft, bituminous coal, which has a low calorific (heat) value but a high ash content. However, coal is plentiful and easily mined. This has led to widespread pollution. During the **apartheid** years, the situation was made worse, because the United Nations banned oil supplies to South Africa. One South African response was to build nuclear power stations. Another was to make oil from coal.

SASOL, a world first

South Africa has the world's biggest coal-to-oil **synthetic fuel** program. Under apartheid, the South African Coal, Oil, and Gas Corporation (SASOL) invented a process to turn solid coal into refined oil in an attempt to beat restrictions on oil imports. The South African government hopes that the SASOL process will

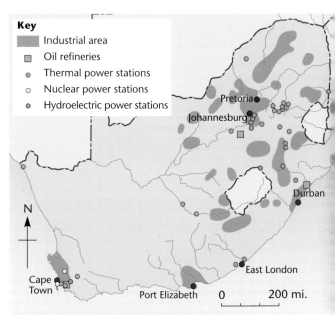

Key
- Industrial area
- Oil refineries
- Thermal power stations
- Nuclear power stations
- Hydroelectric power stations

Locations of Energy Sources in South Africa

	1970	1992
Production	48.5	134.3
Imports	16.6	23.2
Exports	1.8	43.4
Consumption per person	2.2	2.5

(Millions of tons of coal equivalent)
Energy in South Africa, 1970–1992

- help solve the energy problem
- be the foundation of a chemical industry that can compete around the world
- generate thousands of desperately needed jobs

The process by which SASOL makes liquid fuel also produces specialized chemicals. The fuel sells for about $200 a ton, but the chemicals can earn as much as $1,000 a ton. Eventually SASOL hopes to get 50 percent of its income from chemicals.

Despite its successes, there are also problems with this synthetic fuel process.
- It wastes coal and greatly increases carbon emissions.
- Processing synthetic fuels produces concentrated hazardous wastes, as well as sulfur and nitrogen oxides and hydrocarbons.

About 180,000 South Africans work in the chemical industry as a whole, producing 5 percent of the **gross domestic product (GDP)**. The industry could be improved by modernizing and investing in equipment and training its workers. There are also problems, such as high transportation costs that make it difficult to **export** outside of Africa.

For many South Africans, firewood is an important source of energy.

Oil is made at SASOL's energy plant in Sasolburg.

FACT FILE

Energy

South Africa has considerable amounts of energy **resources**, notably coal. However, it lacks oil, and many people have limited access to sufficient energy resources. Coal accounts for about 80 percent of energy consumption, but for many people wood and trash are an important sources of fuel to burn for heat. Coal's uses include the following:

- 52 percent for electricity
- 38 percent for commerce and industry (including synthetic liquid fuels)
- 6 percent for metallurgy
- 3.5 percent to households
- 1 percent for mining and transportation

Renewable forms of energy (such as hydroelectric, solar, and wind) have not been developed very much in South Africa. This is partly because of their cost, and partly because of the abundance and low cost of coal. Less than 5 percent of the country's energy is supplied by renewable forms.

Tourism

▶ Tourism is important to South Africa.
▶ Tourism brings advantages and problems.

International tourism

South Africa is described as "a world in one country." Following the 1994 elections, South Africa has become one of the world's fastest-growing tourist destinations. The majority of visitors are European, although more people are coming from North America.

South Africa's attractions include the Kruger National Park, the scenic beauty of the Cape, hiking trails in the Drakensberg, beaches in Natal, the gold and diamond mines, and, increasingly, tours of Soweto township near Johannesburg.

A government report in 1996 stated that "tourism development in South Africa has largely been a missed opportunity. If South Africa's history had been different, it would probably have been one of the most visited places in the world."

There is still room for expansion of tourism. Income from tourism is from 3 to 4 percent of South Africa's **gross domestic product (GDP)**, compared with a world average of about 11 percent. With gold mining in long-term decline, South Africa is desperately looking for an alternative economic activity to create jobs and bring in much needed foreign money. Tourism has been described as the most promising alternative.

South African tourism still faces big problems.
• There are too few and overcrowded hotels.
• There is a high rate of crime in some areas.

Tourism inequalities

Although tourism benefits South Africa in some ways, it does not benefit everyone equally. Only an estimated 20 percent of black families can afford to take a vacation in South Africa. Also, much of the tourist **infrastructure** (for example,

1990	300,000
1994	700,000
1995	800,000
2000 (est)	1,600,000

Increase in the Number of Foreign Tourists, 1990–2000.

U.K. and Ireland	244,860
Rest of Europe	442,679
North America	124,354
Central and South America	29,037
Australasia	59,951
Asia	129,400
Middle East	20,485
Indian Ocean Islands	11,073
Total	1,071,839

Foreign Visitors to South Africa, 1995

An artificial beach on the south coast attracts tourists.

hotels, airline companies, restaurants) are owned by white rather than black people. Many black people believe that the benefits of tourism go mainly to white people.

Although the government is interested in promoting tourist development, it has chosen to cut the tourism budget to put more money into welfare, education, and housing.

Those in charge of tourism want to develop South Africa as an upscale tourist destination. They do not want tourism to destroy the attractions that tourists come to see. To achieve this, the number of visitors are limited in the Kruger National Park.

Tourists on safari come to see South Africa's animals.

THE KRUGER NATIONAL PARK

The Kruger National Park is one of the most famous of South Africa's attractions. It has more wildlife species than any other park in Africa, due to its variety of habitats. The park has the "big five" animals that people want to see. However, the large number of visitors can be a problem. There is increasing **soil erosion** and litter, mainly due to the number of visitors.

	Number of species
Trees	300
Fish	49
Amphibians	33
Reptiles	114
Birds	507
Mammals	147

Species Diversity in Kruger National Park

The rhino can be seen in Kruger National Park.

FACT FILE

Recent trends in tourism in South Africa
- There was an 11.4 percent increase in the number of foreign tourists to South Africa in 1995.
- The largest increase (120 percent) was in French visitors, following a French advertising campaign.
- South Africa's African visitors are growing slowly (0.5 percent).
- The majority (over 75 percent) of overseas tourists to South Africa are vacation tourists, while business visitors, students, and travelers passing through South Africa make up the remainder.
- The proportion of people visiting South Africa for vacation is increasing.
- In 1995 approximately 4.5 million visitors went to South Africa.

- The relative value of South Africa's main tourist-sources is

U.K.	15%
Germany	14%
France	4%
North America	10%
Asia	9%

Tourism is the world's most important industry— and many countries actively encourage it. Although there are many advantages, such as jobs, investment, and foreign currency, there are serious questions about the environmental and cultural sustainability and acceptability of the increase in tourism.

Private Game Parks in South Africa

▶ Tourism is more profitable than farming.

▶ Trophy hunting on game reserves is profitable, but controversial.

The Tarkuni Estate is located in the southern Kalahari Desert, 80 miles from Kuruman in the Northern Cape. Springbok, a type of small antelope, are common there. But there are also some prized animals such as eland, kudu, and oryx.

Tarkuni Estate is the largest, privately-owned game reserve on the African continent. Its owner, Stephen Boler, is aware that land is becoming increasingly scarce as population increases and that people need more land for agriculture. But in many cases tourism, especially hunting, is more profitable, and it also has a valuable ecological role.

The argument for hunting

The management policy of the Tarkuni Estate is "shoot to **cull** (kill)." Most of its 22,000 acres are given over to wildlife breeding and ecotourism. On the rest of the land, hunters from Europe and North America are invited to pay to kill animals. Different animals have different prices.

For hunters who have flown thousands of miles from Europe or North America, the thrill of the hunt is a great attraction. But it results in the death of a wild animal. For many people, especially observers from the developed world, such killing is just wanton destruction—unnecessary killing for the sake of killing.

As population increases in South Africa, there is more need for farmland. This restricts the amount of land for wild animals. This means that some animals have to be culled in order to avoid overpopulation, which leads to starvation. According to the Tarkuni Estate, it makes sense to let rich foreigners pay for the cost of conservation by letting them do the shooting.

Tarkuni Estate, Northern Cape	
Land area	400 sq. mi., varied terrain for rifle and bow hunting
Animals	40 species of trophy game
Accommodation	3- and 5-star lodging
Staff	includes resident biologist who oversees herd management
Tourist information	located in a disease–free zone, no malaria, has Tarmac runway, free transportation

Facts about the Privately-owned Tarkuni Estate

Jackal	$75
Ostrich	$300
Giraffe	$2,950
Roan (antelope)	$6,500
Buffalo	$6,000
White Rhino	$35,000

Cost of Hunting Wildlife at the Tarkuni Estate

Ecotourism allows tourists to get close to nature.

Relocation involves the movement of wildlife from its natural habitat to a designated area, such as a game park.

Ecotourism

An ecotourist is someone who tries to experience and enjoy nature for its own sake. At nearby Tswalu, ecotourists watch the animals in their natural environment, but they do not try to kill them. On the other hand, many conservation groups agree with culling. For example, the Worldwide Fund for Nature accepts culling (by tourists) provided it is sustainable, scientific, and involves no cruelty. There also must be no available alternative that would better benefit local people.

Trophy hunting earns more money than tourism, which in turn earns more than farming. However, the biggest profit comes from breeding rare animal species and selling surplus animals to other reserves.

FACT FILE

The growth of ecotourism

Ecotourism developed as a form of specialized, flexible tourism. It emerged because mass tourism was seen as having a negative impact upon the natural and social environment. At first, people who took an ecotourism vacation were prepared to accept quite simple accommodations and facilities. This is sustainable and has little effect upon the environment. However, as a location becomes more popular and is marketed more, the number of tourists increases, causing more accommodations and improved facilities to be built. This is an unsustainable form of tourism, because it destroys part of the environment and/or culture that tourists choose to visit.

▶ **South Africa has a favorable balance of trade.**
▶ **South Africa's trade is changing.**

Overseas trade is buying and selling with other countries. **Imports** are the goods and services bought from other countries. **Exports** are the goods and services sold to other countries. The difference between the funds and credit generated by imports and exports is called the **balance of trade**. If a country exports more than it imports, then it earns more than it spends. As of 1996, South Africa had a deficit balance of trade with the three countries with whom it trades the most—the United Kingdom, Germany, and the U.S. South Africa imports more from those countries than it exports to them.

Two of South Africa's main trading partners are **trading blocs, European Union (EU)** and **Southern African Development Community (SADC)**. A trading bloc is a group of countries that agree to have free trade between them, with no restrictions or **tariffs**.

One of South Africa's exports is wine.

South Africa and Southern Africa
The Southern African Development Coordination Conference (SADCC) was formed in 1980 and became the SADC in 1992. South Africa joined the community in 1994. There are now twelve member countries. South Africa has a positive balance of trade with the members of SADC.

South Africa joined SADC because of the advantages of being part of a trading bloc.
• Exporters can reach a bigger market.
• Member countries have more bargaining power because they can act together.
• Imports can be restricted by placing tariffs on imports.

South Africa and the European Union
The Lome Convention is a treaty that governs trade relations between the EU and some of the world's poorest countries. This treaty is due to end in 2000. South Africa does not qualify for preferential trading conditions and European aid granted to other poorer Lome members. Southern European countries, led by Spain, are worried that South African exports would threaten their own agriculture and fisheries.

IMPORTS	million rand
Primary products	
Food	1,060
Inedible raw materials	1,038
Manufactured goods	
Chemicals	3,828
Textiles	781
Metals and metal products	1,371
Machinery	8,476
Motor vehicles	3,082
All other manufactured goods	4,563
Other	4,469
Total	**28,672**

EXPORTS	million rand
Primary products	
Food	2,418
Metal ores	1,185
Diamonds*	3,547
Gold	17,807
Manufactured goods	
Chemicals	1,266
Metals and metal products	4,441
Machinery and transportation equipment	957
Other	12,046
Total	**43,670**

*(excluding industrial diamonds)

South Africa's Imports and Exports, 1994

Imports, 1995	$27 billion

	Percentage of imports
Germany	16
U.S.	16
U.K.	11

Exports, 1995	$27.9 billion

	Percentage of exports
Switzerland	7
U.K.	7
U.S.	5

South Africa's Trading Partners

Products	Rand (billion)	% of total
Nuclear reactors, boilers, machinery	11.8	24.5
Electrical machinery	6.8	14.0
Other unclassified goods	4.3	8.9
Vehicles and parts	4.1	8.6
Chemicals and chemical products	2.7	5.6
Optical, photographic, measuring equipment, etc.	1.9	3.9
Plastics and plastic articles	1.6	3.3
Paper and paperboard	1.1	2.3

South Africa's Industrial Product Exports to EU, 1994

FACT FILE

South Africa and international trade
South Africa is an obvious base for companies that want to take advantage of a regional market containing up to 250 million people.

South Africa is once again part of the southern Africa economic map. Moreover, it has the best transportation and telecommunications **infrastructure** in Africa, it produces more electricity than the rest of Africa put together, and it has one-third of all of Africa's telephone lines.

South Africa's World Trade 1996

Developing the Rural Economy

▶ The informal economy is changing into formal black businesses.
▶ People are carrying out development with very little money.

Although life is difficult for many black people and there is a history of injustice and inequality, there are many ways people have tried to improve their lifestyles and develop their communities.

Informal businesses

The number of businesses owned by black people in South Africa is growing very fast. At first many were small-scale, informal activities, such as selling food, driving taxis, and small-scale manufacturing, such as making bricks. This is called an **informal economy** and is not controlled by strict taxes and laws.

Formal business development

Since the end of **apartheid** and the election of the new government in 1994, the economy has changed. There is a growing black middleclass and many more black managers and industrialists joining the **formal economy**. By 1996 black businesspeople had gained a huge increase in their share of South Africa's economic power. Some white-owned companies were transferred to black owners, and the companies were doing well.

Many businesses, black and white alike, have been affected by conditions outside South Africa. Rising competition and lower **import tariffs** have made foreign goods inexpensive compared with South African goods. This has forced many businesses to close and has caused widespread unemployment.

Taxi operators	100,000
Hawkers (street traders)	150,000
Small shopkeepers	50,000
Small backyard manufacturers	70,000
Others	130,000
Total	500,000

Black-owned Businesses in South Africa, 1995

Community Development in Makua, 1991

There are more opportunities for businesses in

Bricks are made near Glenmore, Eastern Cape.

Key
--- Provincial boundaries
— Main roads
— Railway
✈ Airports

Jane Furse
Makua
Pretoria
Middelburg
Johannesburg
M P U M A L A N G A
G A U T E N G
0   60 mi.

Location of Makua, Northern Province

Intensive commercial development is underway at Keiskammahoek, Eastern Cape.

urban areas than in rural areas, where consumers are very poor. But throughout South Africa there are many attempts by community groups to create jobs, improve living conditions, and encourage sustainable development.

Domestic workers	26%
Gardeners	12%
Seamstresses	8%
Hawking	7%
Taxi driving	7%
Brewing/selling alcohol	5%
Other (laborers, cooks, wood collectors, car washers, bottle collectors, herbalists, hairdressers)	35%

This table lists the main informal employment in South Africa, as a percentage of the total workforce.

This is Dimbaza's central business district.

An example of this is the village of Makua, where the Makua Women's Club decided to overcome the problems of unemployment and the shortage of housing by making bricks. Brick-making is an activity usually controlled by men. At first there was some resistance from local male builders who feared that the women were trying to take over their profitable business. Instead, the women's brick-making has become part of a much wider development process, generating income and providing materials to build new and better housing. It is essential for men and women to work together, rather than against each other.

Soil erosion is another serious problem. Without action to control erosion, future food production would suffer. The Women's Club has organized tree-planting programs. The trees will produce fruit and firewood and reduce soil erosion by wind and water.

One of the main problems is hunger. It is difficult to take action when people are hungry and unmotivated. So the Women's Club has put a lot of work into increasing food production by cultivating more land, planting new seeds, weeding carefully, and increasing the watering of crops. Farming has become more **labor intensive**. The results are impressive. There are new crops of carrots, pumpkins, sweet potatoes, and corn.

One of the main strengths of these projects is that ordinary people carry them out with little money. However, in rural areas, a major problem is that many of the people with initiative and skills have already **migrated** in search of a better life in the city.

FACT FILE

Some common development terms

Bottom-up development involves local communities and local people. It is labor intensive, and there is usually limited funding available. Common projects include building earthen dams and creating cottage industries.

Appropriate development is development that is culturally acceptable, technologically understandable, and economically affordable. It is for and by the community using the community's own resources. It is a type of bottom-up or sustainable form of development.

Sustainable development aims to increase standards of living without destroying the environment and to satisfy basic needs such as food supply and water.

Nongovernment organizations (NGOs) such as Oxfam, Save the Children, and Cafod are mostly charities and are not allied to any political party. NGOs normally work with local communities and small groups, and they help with emergency relief.

5 UNEQUAL REGIONS

Measuring Regional Inequalities

▶ **Development is hard to define.**
▶ **Some aspects are unmeasurable.**
▶ **Levels of development vary across South Africa.**

Development can be about improvements in
- economic growth of the country
- peoples' standards of living
- employment
- health and nutrition
- education
- freedom and human rights
- technology

Most countries, including South Africa, have development inequalities between different regions. South Africa also has striking inequalities between its black and white people.

Some of these contrasts, such as in freedom and human rights, can be difficult to measure. Others aspects of development, for example **gross domestic product (GDP)**, are easier to measure, but do not tell the whole picture.

Key
Rand (billion)
- 0–25
- 26–50
- 51–75
- 76–100
- 101–125
- 126–150

Map of GDP by Province, 1994

South Africa has contrasts in development. This garbage dump is near to the central business district.

Province	Population (million)	GDP per province (billion rand)	GDP per capita (thousand rand)
Northern Province	5.4	14.7	1.9
North West	3.3	21.2	6.5
Gauteng	7.0	144.4	17.5
Mpumalanga	3.0	31.2	9.5
Northern Cape	0.7	80.0	9.2
Free State	2.8	23.7	7.8
KwaZulu-Natal	8.7	57.0	6.0
Western Cape	3.7	53.9	11.3
Eastern Cape	6.5	29.0	3.8

Regional Inequalities as Measured by GDP, 1994

Key
- **Core**
- **Secondary cores**
- **Periphery**

NAMIBIA

BOTSWANA

ZIMBABWE

MOZAMBIQUE

Pretoria •
Johannesburg •

SWAZILAND

LESOTHO

Durban

*INDIAN
OCEAN*

• Cape Town

Port Elizabeth

East London

N

0   250 mi.

Core and Periphery of South Africa

For example, statistical measurements don't include wealth produced in the **informal economy,** or unpaid work. The map on the previous page shows the amounts of GDP in different regions of South Africa.

Core and periphery

One way to understand differences in development between regions is to use the idea of **core** and **periphery**. Core regions are where there is much economic activity, especially industry and business; most of the nation's wealth is concentrated here. South Africa's core region is Gauteng, although there are other **secondary cores**. Away from the cores there are less prosperous areas. This is the periphery. Here there is less economic activity, and incomes and standards of living are lower.

The inequalities in wealth and development between the core regions and the periphery are a severe problem for South Africa. What makes the situation worse is that the core grows and develops at the expense of the periphery.

FACT FILE

Comparative data on race and inequality
These graphs compare the **life expectancy,** purchasing power parity (ppp), and the human development index (HDI) for blacks and whites in South Africa and in the U.S.

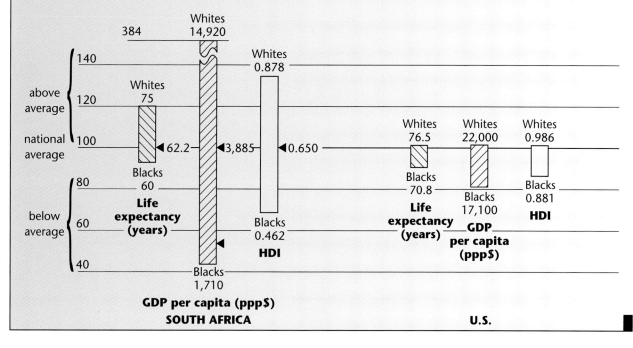

The Core Region

▶ Johannesburg is South Africa's economic core.
▶ Johannesburg was built on the success of the gold mines.

South Africa's core region

South Africa has huge differences in levels of development between its regions. South Africa's **core** region is centered on the Johannesburg area, in Gauteng province. Gauteng covers only 1.5 percent of South Africa's land area, but it produces
- 45 percent of the manufacturing output
- 45 percent of trade
- 55 percent of financial sector earnings
- 30 percent of the country's employment
- 40 percent of the **gross domestic product (GDP)**

A further 30 percent of GDP is produced by the other main cities (**secondary cores**), and together these core and secondary core areas have about one-third of the population.

JOHANNESBURG

Johannesburg is South Africa's most famous and dynamic city, although it is not the capital (which is Pretoria) or the seat of government (which is Cape Town). But Johannesburg is the most important economic center in the country, and is probably the largest and most successful settlement in Africa south of the Sahara. The area contains 20 percent of South Africa's population.

The area around Johannesburg contains the gold-bearing rocks that at one time were the world's richest deposit. The core has been built on this mining success. In the late nineteenth century, earnings from mining were invested in industry and the **infrastructure**.

The size of the gold resource meant that the Johannesburg area developed rapidly. Workers were needed for the fast growing mines and factories; these workers needed homes and spent their wages on other goods. In turn this created more jobs and led to more investment, attracting more workers. This is called the **multiplier effect**. Once started, it was difficult to stop the growth of Johannesburg.

So Johannesburg had an **initial advantage**, its goldfields, but its economy soon grew to include a wide range of industries and services.

Johannesburg is a commercially-active city.

This aerial view is of Johannesburg, South Africa's second largest city.

Today this region is the economic heart of the country. But despite the economic success of Johannesburg and other parts of the core region, there are also problems. Some of these are the result of the core's success. Problems include

- overcrowding in areas such as Hillbrow and Joubert Park
- a shortage of housing, especially low-cost housing
- rapid immigration of young people in search of work
- poor quality housing in the **townships** and central Johannesburg. Up to 2.5 million people live in informal (shanty) housing.
- **segregated** populations, and racial and tribal conflict

Johannesburg has a skyline to rival that of almost any central business district in the world.

FACT FILE

A news reporter looks at life in the core

A mile and a half from Sandton, Johannesburg, is Alexandria. Half a million people live there, squeezed into a square mile and a half. When it rains, the polluted river floods, houses collapse, and the roads turn to mud.

It was stinking and dry, with a flock of aproned women trying to pick up the stranded rubbish. The spick-and-span state of the people's homes is a wonder. On the hills are two great hostels, like prison blocks: one built for men, the other for women. **Apartheid's** planners designed them for a cheap labor pool; everyone else was to be removed. But the people of Alexandria resisted and stayed.

According to some Alexandria residents, most people in Sandton know very little about Alexandria. It is still rare for whites to visit townships.

Source: *The Guardian*, April 11, 1998

South Africa's Periphery

▶ Periphery is outside of the core.
▶ The peripheral regions are underdeveloped.
▶ Improvement has been expensive and difficult.

In some ways, people living in parts of South Africa's **periphery** face problems that are similar to people in peripheral regions in other countries. Incomes and standards of living are low, compared with the **core**. The South African periphery faced special problems under **apartheid** because government policy was to starve the **homelands** of development. These areas are the most underdeveloped part of the periphery, with

- 40 percent of the population
- 13 percent of the land
- 8.3 percent of employment
- 5 percent of the **gross domestic product**

Population problems

The policies of apartheid led to a very uneven age-structure in the homelands. Despite the lack of resources, **population densities** were high. The core's wealth lures young people away. They hope to make a living in the cities. This loss of young people makes it even more difficult to develop the periphery.

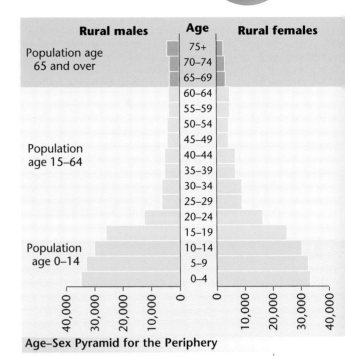

Age–Sex Pyramid for the Periphery

Jobs and the economy

The growing economy in the core acts like a magnet, attracting businesses there. In the periphery, agriculture is underdeveloped and much of the manufacturing is based on textiles and food processing.

Unemployment in the periphery is high. For people who are working in factories, domestic service, and informal occupations, wages can be very low. Many businesses are based on the exploitation of inexpensive labor.

Many parts of the periphery are a very long distance from any large town. Some places are remote and inaccessible.

Many parts of the South African periphery lack substantial development, as shown by the lack of development in Mdantsane's central business district.

The Eastern Cape

The Eastern Cape, an underdeveloped part of the most depressed region in the country, sums up the problems of South Africa's periphery. It has **raw materials**, few towns, and a poor **infrastructure**. It is a long way from the main markets in South Africa. Many people have **migrated** to the core, leaving behind a high proportion of children and elderly.

Plans for development

The South African government's regional development policy plans to offset some of the inequalities between core and periphery. It aims to create jobs by focusing on **industrial development points** in and around the former homelands.

THE MULTIPLIER EFFECT

Once the core began to grow, it attracted more people and economic activities. There were many benefits in locating in the core.
- Closeness to other businesses cut down transportation costs.
- Businesses could sell their products to the growing population.
- There were plenty of workers nearby.

The **multiplier effect** helps explain patterns of migration in South Africa in the 1950s and 1990s. The core region's prosperity and jobs attract migrants from the periphery. These are often young people who are more prepared to move, who then may have children once they get to the city. The core continues to grow and grow.

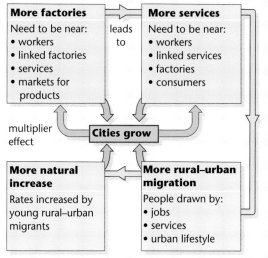

ECONOMY/PEOPLE

More factories
Need to be near:
- workers
- linked factories
- services
- markets for products

leads to

More services
Need to be near:
- workers
- linked services
- factories
- consumers

multiplier effect → **Cities grow**

More natural increase
Rates increased by young rural–urban migrants

More rural–urban migration
People drawn by:
- jobs
- services
- urban lifestyle

Dimbaza was the main site chosen for industrial development in the Eastern Cape. Clothing and textiles, with 60 percent of the jobs, are the most important industries. Much of the workforce is female, especially in textile factories. Wages are very low and often do not provide enough income to support a household.

The government provides **incentives** to attract industries. For example, industries locating in the former homeland of Ciskei get
- moving allowances
- freedom from some taxes, reductions on others
- electricity and transportation grants
- housing subsidies for managers
- grants for each person they employ

In spite of government efforts, industrial development has been expensive and unsuccessful. Many firms closed or moved to the core. The disadvantages were too much.

Unless the government can find other ways of developing the periphery, more black people, especially the young and well-educated, will migrate to big cities. The periphery will then become even less attractive for investors, and regional inequalities will increase even more.

FACT FILE

The Eastern Cape and Dimbaza—an update
In the Eastern Cape most rural people have no choice but to walk more than a mile to get water. Most residents have no sanitation, no electricity, no telephone, and no work.

In Dimbaza 70 percent of the adult population are unemployed. The town is a ghost town. In the center of the town is a children's cemetery, mostly bearing infants who died before the age of two years. In the 1970s heavy storms washed away many of the graves, and little skeletons appeared at the bottom of the hill.

During the 1970s Dimbaza was a "showcase of investment opportunity." However, most of the investments have collapsed or gone elsewhere. Outside one of the few remaining factories, lines of desperate, waiting men and women hope for a few hours of work.

Issues for the Twenty-First Century

▶ **The future holds hope for South Africa's development.**

At the end of the twentieth century, South Africa is changing rapidly and many people wonder how things will change after Nelson Mandela leaves office. The country faces a number of issues.
- Issues within South Africa
- Issues in Southern Africa
- Issues concerning South Africa and the global economy

Issues in South Africa
- Can South Africa tackle racial inequalities in income, welfare, education, housing, and health?
- Can South Africa support its rapidly growing population?
- Where will it find the money to create jobs and housing?
- How will it cope with population growth in the twenty-first century?

In its favor, South Africa has advantages, too.
- It has a talented, innovative population that has moved forward in a spirit of reconciliation since the new government was elected in 1994.
- It has the largest known mineral reserves in Africa.
- It has tremendous opportunities for tourism.
- It has the goodwill of many countries in the world.

South Africa and southern Africa
- Should South Africa concentrate on becoming a superpower in southern Africa, or should it try to resolve its own problems within the country?
- Could a southern African **trading bloc** become as important as the **European Union**?
- Would a trading bloc give the countries of southern Africa a more powerful say in world politics?
- South Africa is the richest country in southern Africa. Will it have to spend money on its neighbors rather than on its own people?

Thabo Nbeki and President Nelson Mandela stand next to former president, F. W. de Klerk.

- Should South Africa compete with its neighboring countries or cooperate with them?

South Africa has the political, economic, and financial resources to help shape the future of southern Africa. Its leaders are experienced negotiators and have shown how it is possible to overcome decades of **discrimination**.

The new South African government has tried to follow a **capitalist** form of development that continues to create wealth rather than just spread it out. But there may be difficult choices. Create wealth or tackle inequalities?

South Africa is a rainbow nation.

South Africa and the world

- Is South Africa a developed country or a less developed country?
- Should South Africa receive aid to help it develop?
- How can South Africa develop in a sustainable way?
- Should South Africa benefit from its large, low-paid workforce and try to attract international companies?

South Africa's economy has two parts—a small developed sector and a less-developed, larger sector. This means that the country has experience and know-how, but this needs to be shared throughout the country.

South Africa participates in the Olympics.

South Africa is entitled to foreign aid. However, healthy trade is more important and more long-term, and South Africa has a healthy trading pattern.

With a rapidly growing population, especially in overcrowded rural areas, South Africa has to adopt more sustainable practices. Years of discrimination have forced people to develop survival techniques. These can be developed into sustainable forms of agriculture, soil conservation, and water conservation and will be another important basis for development in the twenty-first century.

South Africa is attractive to international companies because of its inexpensive labor force. But South Africa needs to build up industries for the twentieth-first century based on people's skills.

FACT FILE

South Africa's achievements
South Africa's government has made two main achievements since achieving power in 1994. They are political stability and determination to follow conservative economic policies rather than redistributing much of South Africa's wealth to the underclass. Now the government needs to deregulate, open the economy to private investors, and create a better image of South Africa abroad.

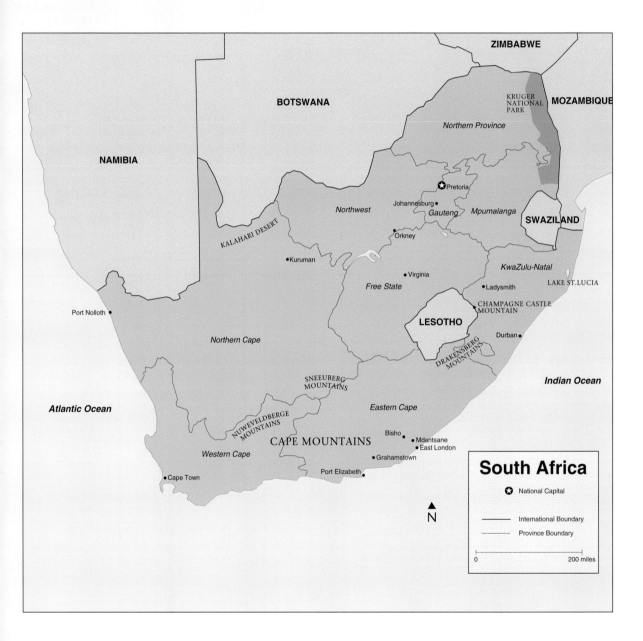

ZIMBABWE

BOTSWANA

KRUGER NATIONAL PARK

MOZAMBIQUE

Northern Province

NAMIBIA

Pretoria

Johannesburg •

Northwest

Gauteng

Mpumalanga

SWAZILAND

KALAHARI DESERT

• Orkney

• Kuruman

• Virginia

KwaZulu-Natal

LAKE ST.LUCIA

• Ladysmith

Free State

CHAMPAGNE CASTLE MOUNTAIN

Port Nolloth •

LESOTHO

Durban •

Northern Cape

DRAKENSBERG MOUNTAINS

SNEEUBERG MOUNTAINS

Indian Ocean

Atlantic Ocean

Eastern Cape

NUWEVELDBERGE MOUNTAINS

Bisho •

• Mdantsane

CAPE MOUNTAINS

• East London

• Grahamstown

Western Cape

Port Elizabeth •

• Cape Town

N

South Africa

⭐ National Capital

International Boundary

Province Boundary

0   200 miles

More Books to Read

Bradley, Catherine. *The End of Apartheid.* Chatham, NJ: Raintree Steck-Vaughn Publishers. 1995.

Brothers, Don. *South Africa.* Broomal, PA: Chelsea House Publishers. 1989.

Flint, David. *South Africa.* Chatham, NJ: Raintree Steck-Vaughn Publishers. 1996.

Halliburton, Warren J. *African Industries.* Parsippany, NJ: Silver Burdett Press. 1993.

Kizilos, Peter. *South Africa: In the Midst of Change.* Minneapolis, MN: Lerner Publishing Group. 1998.

Lowis, Peter. *South Africa.* Chatham, NJ: Raintree Steck-Vaughn. 1996.

Meisel, Jacqueline D. *South Africa at the Crossroads.* Brookfield, CT: Millbrook Press. 1994.

Middleton, Nick. *Southern Africa.* Raintree Steck-Vaughn Publishers. 1995.

Pratt, Paula B. *The End of Apartheid in South Africa.* San Diego, CA: Lucent Books. 1995.

Smith, Chris. *Conflict in Southern Africa.* New York: Simon & Schuster Children's. 1993.

Glossary

Note: The names of mountain ranges in maps are reproduced here in the original Afrikaans, where no convention exists for an English translation. Thus, the Afrikaans word *berg* (sing.) or *berge* (pl.) literally means "mountain(s)."

accessibility the centrality of a location; how easy is it to reach

adult literacy the percentage of adults that can read and write

altitude height of the land. It has an important influence on climate, vegetation, and agriculture.

apartheid a system of racial **discrimination** whereby the white minority had large advantages over the black population. The apartheid system created **homelands** for blacks. There was also discrimination at an urban level (**townships**) and at a small-scale level (facilities were **segregated**)

apartheid city a city divided both geographically and socially along the lines of **apartheid**

balance of trade the balance between a country's **exports** and **imports**. A positive balance means that exports are greater than imports.

birth rate the number of live births per thousand population

bushveld a type of vegetation consisting of bushes, small trees, and grass

capitalist economic system based on private ownership of land and production, using hired labor, and producing goods and services that are offered on the free market

check-dam small-scale earth or stone dam usually built by a local community to hold water and prevent **soil erosion**

colonists the earliest overseas **migrants** who moved into an area

colony a country that has been taken under the political and economic control of another country

commercial farm farm that produces goods to sell in order to make a profit

condense conversion of moisture from a gas to a liquid

convection storm thunderstorm caused by the rising of warm air

core the economic center of the counry; vibrant, rich in **resources**, and showing growth, compared with a disadvantaged, depressed **periphery**, lacking in resources and growth

cull controlled killing of animals to keep their numbers down

death rate the number of deaths per thousand of population

deforestation removal of trees (and other vegetation) for farming, fuelwood, and timber **resources**

desertification the spread of desert conditions into nondesert areas

diguette small-scale dam

discrimination unequal treatment; favoritism for some but injustice for others

distribution where things are located/found

drought a long-term decline in water availability

dustbowl dry land where dust storms are common

emigrated left one's country or region to live in another

European Union (EU) a group of 15 countries in Western Europe with close economical and political links. The EU is a major trading partner with South Africa.

export good or services that is sold by one country to another

formal economy the official part of the economy; businesses governed by laws and regulation

gross domestic product (GDP) the value of goods produced in a country over a year

gross national product (GNP) the value of goods produced in a country over a year, plus income from services, tourism, investment, and so on

gully steep, narrow, deep channel created by water flowing over a surface

Highveld see veld

homeland area set aside for black people under apartheid. Most were **peripheral**, isolated, and fragmented pieces of land with very high **population density**

humid areas that are wet

hydroelectric power (HEP) the use of water to generate power

immigrant person who moves into an area or country

imports goods and services that one country buys from another

incentive attraction such as money, grants, factories, and subsidies provided by the government to attract industry

industrial development points areas for industrial growth, located in the former **homelands** and/or distant from the main metropolitan areas

infant mortality rate (IMR) the number of deaths of infants under the age of one year per thousand live births

influx control policies aimed at controlling the movement of black people and their number in **urban** areas

informal economy unofficial jobs and businesses, such as domestic work, gardening, operating taxis, and selling food

infrastructure the human-built environment; includes roads, railroads, housing, factories, and water and energy supplies

initial advantage a feature, such as a raw material, that gives a location an advantage over other areas

irrigation process of supplying water to dry farm land

labor intensive use of human labor rather than machinery to perform a task, such as for farming or industry

latitude the position of a place north or south of the equator

life expectancy the number of years that a person is expected to live

location another term for township

longitude the position of a place east or west of Greenwich (London)

Mediterranean climate a climate with warm, wet winters and hot, dry summers

migrant worker worker who worked away from home in mines and factories. They were often away from home for up to a year.

migrated/migration a change in permanent residence

Minimum Living Level a level below which it is impossible to live/survive

multiplier effect the process where a growth area attracts investment and **migrants** and improves its advantages; also known as cumulative causation

natural hazard natural event that endangers the loss of life, property, or livelihood

Glossary, *continued*

natural increase population growth in which **birth rates** are greater than **death rates**

neonatal the first four weeks of life

newly industrialized country (NIC) country with a high percentage of the workforce employed in manufacturing, and a high percentage of **exports** from manufacturing

overgrazed loss of vegetation eaten by domestic and wild animals

payment in kind payment on farms by food or wine rather than wages

perception what people believe exists, rather than what actually exists

perinatal from the fourth week after conception to the first week after birth

periphery on the edge; away from the center

peri-urban a large sprawling settlement lacking in jobs and basic services; usually located on the edge of an **urban** area

pesticide chemical used to destroy pests

plateau an area of flat land at high **altitude**

population composition a description of the population, normally the age–sex structure

population densities the number of people per square mile; tells how many people in an area

population distribution the actual location of people; where they are

population pressure the stresses placed upon the enviroment (and **resources**) by population growth

post-apartheid city the new **urban** form resulting from the collapse of the **apartheid** system

productivity a measure of how much is produced; commonly used in farming (yields/acre) or industry

raw material any natural **resource** that can be used, such as gold, coal, cotton

relief the effect of the altitude (height) or topography (shape) of the land

relief rainfall rain that is formed when air is forced to rise over high ground

reserve rural area set aside by whites for black people to live in. These were **peripheral**, less-developed parts of South Africa, away from economic centers. Later, they became **homelands**.

resettlement plan the forced removal of black people and their resettlement in **homelands** and **peri-urban** areas. This was a policy of the **apartheid** era.

resource anything that is valuable, for example, gold, soil, diamonds, water, land

run-off rain water and flash floods that run over the land's surface

sanctions impositions put on a country by other countries in order to pressure a country into reform

secondary core important **urban** industrial area, but not as dominant as the main **core** area

segregation the enforced separation of people of different races

semi-arid/semi-arid area area receiving about 14–20 inches of rain each year with seasonal **drought**

soil degradation a decline in the quantity (amount) or quality (fertility) of soil

soil erosion the removal of soil by water and wind at a rate greater than soil is being created

South African Development Community (SADC) a collection of countries in Southern Africa with close economic and trade links

subsistence farm farm that grows food for own needs and not to sell

subtropical latitudes around 25°–35° either side of the equator

synthetic fuel fuels made by the conversion of one material to another, such as from coal to oil

tariff tax placed upon **imports** to make them more expensive and make home goods more competitive

township separate area of generally low-quality housing reserved for black, colored, or Asian people

toxic poisonous

toxic heavy metal concentrations of toxic metal in the soil; for example, lead, zinc, mercury, cadmium

trading bloc a group of countries combined for the purpose of buying and selling to each other and buying and selling together as a group

urban/urbanized where many people live in large built-up areas, with a high proportion of manufacturing and service jobs

urbanization an increase in the proportion of population living in **urban** or **peri-urban** areas

veld grassland

vlei(s) grassland

Index

Bold type refers to terms included in the glossary.